GOD'S CRIME SCENE

SCENE

PARTICIPANT'S GUIDE

A COLD-CASE DETECTIVE
EXAMINES THE EVIDENCE FOR A
DIVINELY CREATED UNIVERSE

J. WARNER
WALLACE

DAVID C COOK

transforming lives together

GOD'S CRIME SCENE PARTICIPANT'S GUIDE
Published by David C Cook
4050 Lee Vance Drive
Colorado Springs, CO 80918 U.S.A.

Integrity Music Limited, a Division of David C Cook
Brighton, East Sussex BN1 2RE, England

The graphic circle C logo is a registered trademark of David C Cook.

Details in some stories have been changed to protect the identities of the persons involved.

All Scripture quotations are taken from the New American Standard Bible®, copyright ©
1960, 1995 by The Lockman Foundation. Used by permission. (www.Lockman.org).

ISBN 978-0-8307-7660-3
eISBN 978-0-8307-7661-0

© 2019 James Warner Wallace
Published in association with the literary agency of Mark Sweeney & Associates, Naples, FL 34113.

Illustrations by J. Warner Wallace
The Team: Stephanie Bennett, Amy Konyndyk, Jack Campbell, Susan Murdock
Cover Design: Nick Lee
Cover Photo: ESO/Igor Chekalin

Printed in the United States of America
First Edition 2019

1 2 3 4 5 6 7 8 9 10

051619

CONTENTS

IN THE BEGINNING

Was the Universe an Inside Job?

As a homicide detective, I've been dispatched to a variety of death scenes over the years. But not every *death* scene is a *crime* scene. There are four ways to die and only one of them is criminal: *murder*. So how do homicide detectives tell the difference between natural deaths, accidents, suicides, and homicides? We ask one simple question: Can we explain everything we find *in the room* by staying *in the room* for an explanation?

If there's no evidence of an outside intruder, the best inference is usually a natural death, an accident, or a suicide. If, on the other hand, we have evidence *in the room* that indicates someone *other* than the inhabitant (someone *outside the room*) is responsible, we must at least consider the reasonable inference of a homicide. When there's evidence of an *intruder*, our priorities shift toward *murder*.

What if we applied this simple "inside or outside the room" approach to the entire natural universe? Can we explain everything we see (and experience) in the universe by staying *inside* the natural universe for an explanation? Can space, time, and matter, governed by the laws of physics and chemistry, explain everything we find in the universe, or is there a better explanation *outside the material realm*?

Several features of the universe require explanation. Over the course of this study, we'll examine eight attributes of the cosmos, studying explanations that are offered from inside and outside the "room" of the natural universe. We'll investigate the cosmos like a crime scene, using the skills of a detective, to determine if the universe is God's "crime scene."

We'll begin where all good detectives begin, by examining *causes*. In homicide investigations, detectives ask, "Who caused this murder?" "What motivated this suspect to commit this crime?"

Criminal investigations are largely *causal* investigations. Detectives learn to ask good questions about causation to determine the identity of a suspect. Judges then instruct jurors about causation to help them render a verdict. Here's an example from the State of California Jury Instructions:

> *An act causes [an injury] if the [injury] is the direct, natural, and probable con-*
> *sequence of the act and the [injury] would not have happened without the act. A*
> *natural and probable consequence is one that a reasonable person would know is*
> *likely to happen if nothing unusual intervenes. In deciding whether a consequence*
> *is natural and probable, consider all the circumstances established by the evidence.*

In this session, we'll examine the issue of *causation* as we ask the following questions: "Did the universe have a beginning?" "If so, what caused the universe to begin?" "What is the nature of this 'first cause'?" We'll investigate the evidence to determine if the beginning of the universe was "likely to happen if nothing *unusual* intervene[d]."

OPEN THE CASE FILE
(5 MINUTES – CONSIDER AND ANSWER AS MANY QUESTIONS AS POSSIBLE)

How would you define the word *miracle*?

_____

_____

_____

Many people are hesitant to believe what the New Testament says about Jesus because the Gospels include miraculous claims. Why do you think people are hesitant to accept miracles?

_____

_____

_____

Have you ever thought about the origin of the universe? The apostle John wrote the following in the book of Revelation:

Worthy are You, our Lord and our God, to receive glory and honor and power; for You created all things, and because of Your will they existed, and were created. (4:11)

Why would the act of creation make God worthy of worship?

_____

_____

_____

What difference would it make if the universe had a *beginning*, rather than having existed *eternally*?

_____

_____

_____

VIEW THE VIDEO TESTIMONY
(11 MINUTES – TAKE NOTES AND FILL IN THE DIAGRAM)

Understanding the "inside or outside the room" principle

_____

_____

_____

Applying the "inside or outside the room" principle to the universe

_____

_____

_____

Examining the evidence that demonstrates our universe had a beginning

_____

_____

_____

_____

_____

Fill in the missing words in the following diagram based on the information J. Warner provided in the video:

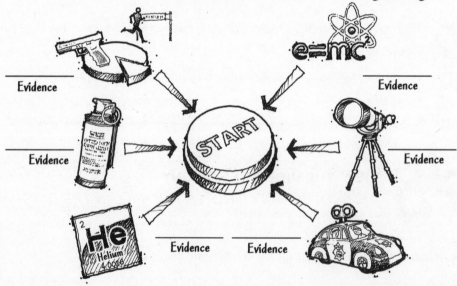

The Diverse, Cumulative Case for a Beginning

Evidence

Evidence

Evidence

Evidence

Evidence   Evidence

Examining one attempt to avoid a universe that has a beginning (from Lawrence Krauss)

_____

_____

_____

Understanding why the beginning of space, time, and matter requires a cause *outside* the "room" of the universe

_____

_____

_____

CONDUCT A GROUP INVESTIGATION
(23 MINUTES – INVESTIGATE THE ISSUES AND ANSWER THE QUESTIONS)

Read aloud the following paragraphs describing ways scientists try to explain the expansion of our universe to avoid a *beginning*, then answer the related questions:

 Could the Universe Be Expanding Eternally?

Models like the Steady State Theory claim the universe has been expanding and "filling in" *eternally* without a point of origin. But this theory lacks evidential support and fails to explain the existence of cosmic background radiation and the overabundance of helium in the universe.

 Why do you think some scientists are trying to avoid the inference that the universe had a beginning?

 A Tool for the Call-Out Bag:

HOW CAN WE SPOT BAD EXPLANATIONS?

Alternative explanations are offered in every criminal trial, but we can identify three characteristics of bad explanations to disqualify them quickly:

1. The explanation is not supported by the evidence

2. The explanation attempts to errantly redefine the facts of the case

3. The explanation is logically contradictory

When one of these three liabilities is identified in an argument, the explanation offered is either inferior or fallacious.

_____

_____

Look at the "Tool for the Call-Out Bag" box (previous page). From which of the three descriptions of "bad explanations" does the Steady State Theory seem to suffer?

_____

_____

Could the Universe Be Cycling Eternally between Expansion and Contraction?

Oscillating or cyclical theories claim the universe has been expanding and contracting *eternally* and account for our current expansion as a temporary condition preceding another period of contraction. But there isn't enough *mass* in the universe for gravity to slow its expansion (to cause a contraction cycle). These theories have not replaced the Standard Cosmological Model that J. Warner described because they are extremely speculative and rely on highly controversial String Theory physics.

Physicist Andrei Linde wrote that one of the cyclical theories, the Cyclic Ekpyrotic Scenario, is "very popular among journalists" but is "rather unpopular among scientists," based on its highly speculative nature.[1] Why do you think scientists are willing to entertain theories that are not supported strongly by evidence?

_____

_____

Could the Universe Be Part of a Larger, Eternal Environment?

Quantum theories, like the one offered by Lawrence Krauss (and described by J. Warner in the video), argue that our universe emerged from subatomic "virtual particles" in a preexisting, eternal quantum vacuum. As J. Warner mentioned, however, these models redefine the meaning of "nothing," borrowing space, time, and matter (before it even exists) to account for preexisting (1) primordial vacuum, (2) virtual particles, and (3) time required for our universe to emerge.

Look once again at the "Tool for the Call-Out Bag" box. From which of the three descriptions of bad explanations does Lawrence Krauss's theory seem to suffer?

_____

5 Can you rearticulate why this theory doesn't explain how the universe came into being?

_____

Examine the following diagram based on the evidence J. Warner described in the video and the alternative explanations outlined in this participant's guide. Fill in the reasons why the alternative explanations don't work:

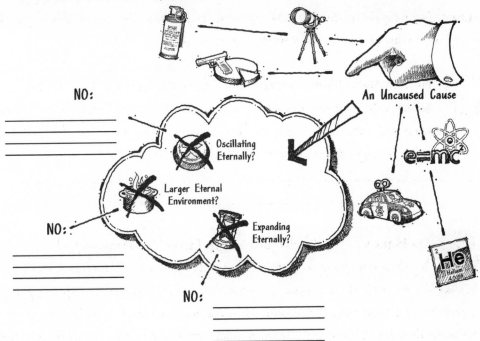

"Inside the Room" or "Outside the Room"
The Weakness of Internal Explanations Compared to the Strength of External Explanations

An Uncaused Cause

NO:
_____
_____
_____

Oscillating Eternally?

Larger Eternal Environment?

NO:
_____
_____

Expanding Eternally?

NO:
_____
_____
_____

 6 As the diagram indicates, the alternative explanations would allow scientists to explain the existence of the cosmos from _inside_ the "room" of the natural universe by using nothing more than space, time, matter, physics, and chemistry. But if all the evidence indicates the universe has a beginning, what is the most reasonable explanation for the *cause* of the universe? Why must this cause be outside the "room" as illustrated in the diagram?

_____

_____

 Like most of my criminal investigations, each piece of evidence from the crime scene ("inside the room") will tell us something about the potential existence and nature of a causal suspect ("outside the room").

A Tool for the Call-Out Bag:

WHAT IS THE NATURE OF OUR "SUSPECT"?

Given what we know so far, the cause of the universe is:

1. external to the _____

2. non_____, atemporal, and non_____

3. uncaused

4. powerful enough to create everything we see in the _____

The origin of the universe is an important piece of evidence pointing to the existence of an external cause, a particular sort of "suspect." As we examine the evidence related to this cause, we can begin to organize a "suspect" profile.

In the sidebar, fill-in the "Suspect" Profile we've assembled so far.

 TAKE A PERSONAL ASSESSMENT
(5 MINUTES OR MORE – EXAMINE YOUR OWN SITUATION AND ANSWER THE QUESTIONS)

Have you ever doubted the existence of miracles? Have you ever been skeptical when someone claimed a miracle occurred in his or her life? Describe the times when you have doubted descriptions of miracles:

_____

_____

_____

_____

Think about the many miracles described in the Old and New Testaments. Which miracle seems the most amazing (or even improbable)?

_____

_____

_____

 Now read Genesis 1:1. Why is this miracle, performed by God, the most amazing miracle of all? If a Divine Being created everything from nothing, how might this truth help you overcome any personal skepticism you might have about "lesser" miracles described in the New Testament?

_____

_____

_____

 ## FORM A STRATEGIC PLAN
(5 MINUTES – EXAMINE YOUR CALENDAR AND CREATE AN ACTION PLAN)

 Is there someone in your life who loves science and doubts the existence of God? List a few people who fit this description:

_____

_____

_____

 Are you prepared to discuss the scientific evidence with people like those you've just listed? Make a strategic plan. First, set a date range to explore the evidence. Here are a couple of books to help you examine the evidence:

God's Crime Scene: A Cold-Case Detective Examines the Evidence for a Divinely Created Universe by J. Warner Wallace

On Guard: Defending Your Faith with Reason and Precision by William Lane Craig

Set a date range to read these (or other similar) books to better understand the evidence: _____. Now set a date when you will begin to discuss the evidence with someone you described at the beginning of this section: _____.

MAKE A CLOSING STATEMENT
(1 MINUTE – CONTEMPLATE AND PRAY)

The beginning of the universe cannot be explained from "inside the room." The evidence points to a cause *outside* of space, time, and matter. Cosmologist Paul Davies, recognizing the dilemma presented by the evidence, wrote, "One might consider some supernatural force, some agency beyond space and time as being responsible … or one might prefer to regard the [beginning of the universe] as an event without a cause. It seems to me that we don't have too much choice. Either … something *outside* of the physical world … or … an event without a cause."[2] This inference of a cause "outside the room" is reasonable, given the evidence we've examined in this session, including the weakness of the alternative explanations.

God, we are in awe of Your powerful work in creation. You are the uncaused Cause of the universe and everything in it. Scientific findings indicate that our universe had a beginning. The evidence for a creator supports the biblical definition of You as an all-powerful, nonspatial, atemporal, and nonmaterial Creator. We thank You for giving us life and purpose, and for the abundance of evidence that points to Your existence. In Jesus's name we pray, amen.

CONDUCT A SECONDARY INVESTIGATION
(READ ON YOUR OWN FOR BETTER UNDERSTANDING)

To better understand the issues raised in this session, read *God's Crime Scene* chapter 1, "In the Beginning: Was the Universe an Inside Job?" For an in-depth discussion of all the alternative scientific theories, read the Secondary Investigation section of *God's Crime Scene*, taking notes specifically on chapter 1 (pages 205–13).

_____

_____

_____

_____

_____

_____

_____

_____

_____

_____

_____

_____

_____

Session Two
TAMPERING WITH THE EVIDENCE
Who Is Responsible?

Helen knew something was wrong when her daughter Carrie failed to answer the door. Carrie said she'd be home, and her car was parked in the driveway. However, Helen noticed Carrie's curtains were unusually drawn. Carrie never locked the back door, yet Helen found the door locked and all the windows closed. Helen began to panic. She knew Todd and Carrie had a tumultuous marriage, one that included physical violence. And even though Todd had moved out, Helen still feared for her daughter's safety. The couple had a child named Lexi, but the violence had only intensified since her birth.

When Helen couldn't get Carrie to answer the door, she decided to call the police. Our officers responded and approached the rear of the house. Immediately after smelling gas, they called in the Fire Department Hazmat Team. Upon entering the house, the team discovered Carrie and her infant daughter lying in bed in the upstairs master bedroom. Autopsies would later reveal they asphyxiated as the gas level in the home rose above the oxygen level.

I arrived on the scene and discovered the second-floor hallway was littered with dirty clothing and the laundry basket at the top

Cold-Case Approach:

HOW DO LAYERED EVIDENCES HELP US EVALUATE ALLEGED COINCIDENCES?

When many layers of evidence uniformly point to the activity of a particular suspect, this suspect must be considered the most reasonable inference.

The larger the number of conditions in each layer of evidence, the less likely the conditions are coincidental (and the more reasonable the inferences).

In this session, we'll examine layered evidences to determine the existence and nature of an external "suspect."

of the stairwell was empty. The door to the master bedroom was closed when officers arrived, and a pile of laundry was lying against the bottom of the door. The home's antiquated heater was mounted to the wall separating the bedroom from the upstairs hallway. Searching further, I noticed the pilot light was out but the gas valve was set in the open position. The vents on the bedroom side of the heater were also open, though the hallway vents were closed.

As part of the follow-up investigation, we discovered the gas company had turned off the gas service for lack of payment, but two days earlier, Todd had paid to restart the service. We decided to investigate this as a homicide. There were simply too many coincidences. The more we examined the layers of evidence, the more it appeared to be a crime scene. The only occupants of the house, Carrie and Lexi, did not appear to be responsible for the conditions we found inside. The weathered windows were shut, the laundry was blocking the door from the hallway, and the heater valve was open. According to Helen, Carrie would never have allowed—not to mention *caused*—these conditions. We had good reason to believe someone *outside* the house had *rigged* the conditions *inside* the house to cause the outcome.

Like this murder scene, there are layers of "conditions" in the universe that require explanation. The foundational laws of physics, the regional properties of our solar system, and the locational conditions of our planet are "fine-tuned" with incredible precision to allow for the existence of *life*. If circumstances had been just slightly different in Carrie's house, no one would have *died* that night. In a similar way, if circumstances were just slightly different in our universe, no one would be *alive* today.

The *just so* appearance of fine-tuning in our universe is another piece of evidence that must be explained from *inside* or *outside* the "room." This fine-tuning is rather uncontroversial among scientists and cosmologists, even though few agree on the existence of an external Fine-Tuner. In this session, we'll examine this piece of evidence to determine if someone *outside* the room "rigged" the conditions *inside* the universe to cause the outcome.

OPEN THE CASE FILE
(5 MINUTES – CONSIDER AND ANSWER AS MANY QUESTIONS AS POSSIBLE)

1. Imagine buying a new car and discovering on your *first drive* that the radio was tuned to your favorite stations and your favorite snacks were in the center console. What would you assume?

_____

_____

_____

2. What difference would it make if the entire universe had been prepared for you *in advance?*

_____

_____

_____

3. Read Psalm 8:3–4:

When I consider Your heavens, the work of Your fingers, the moon and the stars, which You have ordained; what is man that You take thought of him, and the son of man that You care for him?

What does this verse tell us about the heart that God has for His creation? What, specifically, does this tell us about God's heart for *humans*?

_____

_____

_____

VIEW THE VIDEO TESTIMONY
(10 MINUTES – TAKE NOTES)

Understanding the layers of evidence investigated in crime scenes

Layered Evidence of Tampering

UNLIKELY Conditions

UNIQUE Backstory

Locational

RARE Circumstances

Regional

Foundational

_____

_____

_____

Investigating the layered fine-tuning of the universe

Foundational fine-tuning of physics:

_____

_____

_____

Foundational Fine-Tuning

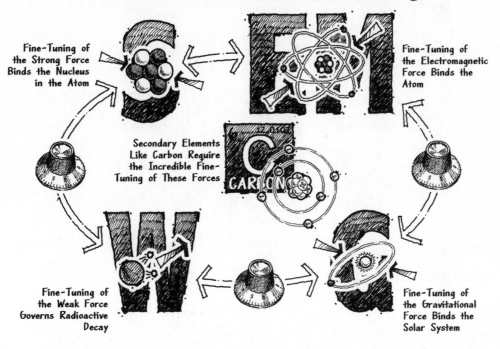

Fine-Tuning of the Strong Force Binds the Nucleus in the Atom

Fine-Tuning of the Electromagnetic Force Binds the Atom

Secondary Elements Like Carbon Require the Incredible Fine-Tuning of These Forces

CARBON

Fine-Tuning of the Weak Force Governs Radioactive Decay

Fine-Tuning of the Gravitational Force Binds the Solar System

Regional fine-tuning of our galaxy and solar system:

_____

_____

_____

Regional Fine-Tuning

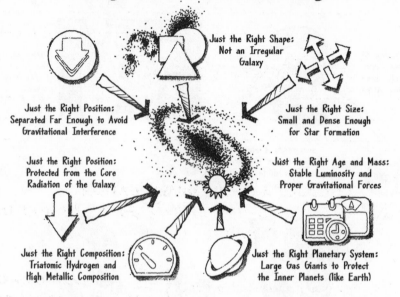

Just the Right Shape:
Not an Irregular
Galaxy

Just the Right Position:
Separated Far Enough to Avoid
Gravitational Interference

Just the Right Size:
Small and Dense Enough
for Star Formation

Just the Right Position:
Protected from the Core
Radiation of the Galaxy

Just the Right Age and Mass:
Stable Luminosity and
Proper Gravitational Forces

Just the Right Composition:
Triatomic Hydrogen and
High Metallic Composition

Just the Right Planetary System:
Large Gas Giants to Protect
the Inner Planets (like Earth)

Locational fine-tuning of our planet:

_____

_____

_____

Locational Fine-Tuning

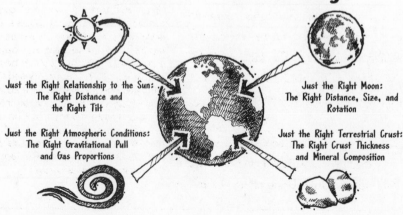

Just the Right Relationship to the Sun:
The Right Distance and
the Right Tilt

Just the Right Moon:
The Right Distance, Size, and
Rotation

Just the Right Atmospheric Conditions:
The Right Gravitational Pull
and Gas Proportions

Just the Right Terrestrial Crust:
The Right Crust Thickness
and Mineral Composition

Inferring the existence of a Fine-Tuner

_____

_____

_____

Examining one explanation for fine-tuning: the "multiverse"

_____

_____

_____

 CONDUCT A GROUP INVESTIGATION
(25 MINUTES – INVESTIGATE THE ISSUES AND ANSWER THE QUESTIONS)

Read aloud the following paragraphs describing ways scientists try to explain the fine-tuning of the cosmos by staying *inside* the "room" of our universe, then answer the related questions:

 **Is Fine-Tuning *Unrequired*?**

Some physicists deny the importance of fine-tuning by claiming life could have emerged from broader, less fine-tuned parameters. However, they typically *redefine* the nature of "life" to accomplish this. The kind of "life" described by those who hold this position is decidedly different from life as we know it.

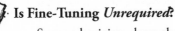 Refer back to the "bad explanations" described in session 1. Which one of the bad explanations is being offered here?

A Tool for the Call-Out Bag:

WHAT ROLE DOES PATIENCE PLAY IN ASSEMBLING AN EVIDENTIAL CASE?

Police work has been described as hours of boredom punctuated by moments of stressful urgency. This is particularly true for patrol assignments, but it's also true of criminal investigations.

Detectives often spend hundreds of hours investigating clues and collecting seemingly meaningless pieces of evidence before they are able to see the big picture. In the early hours and days of an investigation, it's important to be patient and thorough. As we assembled the layered evidence surrounding Carrie's and Lexi's deaths, the reasonable inference of tampering became clear. In a similar way, we must patiently collect the evidence in the universe before we can make a reasonable inference about the fine-tuning of the universe.

Is Fine-Tuning the Result of *Chance*?

Some have argued the fine-tuning of the universe is simply an *accident*. But this explanation is logically inconsistent with the purpose of any scientific investigation (to push beyond the appearance of coincidence to find an explanation), and it completely ignores the *improbability* of the evidence we've described.

 Imagine telling Carrie's mother that all the layered evidences at the crime scene were simply coincidences. Why would this response be unsatisfying to Carrie's family? Why should "coincidence" also be unsatisfying when explaining the fine-tuning of the universe?

_____

_____

_____

Is Fine-Tuning the Result of *Physical Necessity*?

Some cosmologists believe the universe is the way it is because the laws of physics do not *allow any alternative* (if the laws of nature are *fixed* and *inflexible*, no other versions of these laws are *possible*). But this explanation is *not* supported by evidence. There is no reason to believe the laws of nature could not have been *different*, and even if the foundational laws of the universe were fixed, this would fail to explain the regional and locational fine-tuning we've described.

Read Romans 1:20:

For since the creation of the world His invisible attributes, His eternal power and divine nature, have been clearly seen, being understood through what has been made, so that they are without excuse.

If the laws of physics we observe in the universe are simply the reflection of one of God's "invisible attributes," what does this tell us about the nature of God?

_____

_____

_____

Is Fine-Tuning an *Observational Phenomenon*?

Some scientists believe we observe fine-tuning because, if *not* for such fine-tuning, we wouldn't be here to observe the universe *in the first place*. Physicist Lawrence Krauss once said, "Put another way, it is not too surprising to find that we live in a universe in which we can live!"[1] This explanation makes yet another logical error (confusing an *observation* for an *explanation*) while ignoring the inferences of fine-tuning.

Imagine telling Carrie's mother, "It's not too surprising to find a dead body in a house filled with gas!" Why would this *observation* be unsatisfying to Carrie's family as an *explanation*? Why should it also be unsatisfying when explaining the fine-tuning of the universe?

_____

_____

_____

Is Fine-Tuning a Consequence of the *Multiverse*?

To some physicists, the multiverse has the best chance of explaining the appearance of fine-tuning in our universe. But these theories lead to the absurdities J. Warner mentioned in the video. More importantly, multiverse explanations point to an *external* causal agent—a "multiverse generator" of sorts—outside of space, time, and matter.

Refer to your notes from the session video to describe why multiverse explanations are unreasonable:

_____

_____

_____

Look at the following diagram of the ways secular scientists try to explain fine-tuning without invoking a Divine "Fine-Tuner."

Internal vs. External Explanations

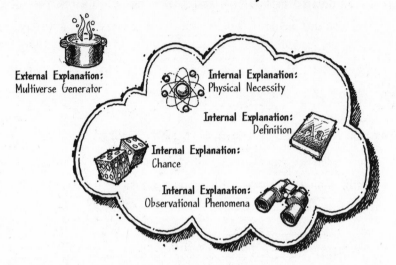

 When scientists offer a multiverse generator, they assume it has spatial, material, and temporal properties. Why is this assumption unreasonable, given that the multiverse generator would have to be *outside* the spatial, material, and temporal "room" of the universe?

_____

_____

_____

 TAKE A PERSONAL ASSESSMENT
(4 MINUTES – EXAMINE YOUR OWN SITUATION AND ANSWER THE QUESTIONS)

It's quite possible that, prior to this session, you've never considered the powerful evidence of fine-tuning in the universe. How might you explain this evidence to others? Examine the following diagram and do your best to describe why the secular explanations for fine-tuning fail. Then describe why the inference of a Divine Fine-Tuner is the most reasonable explanation:

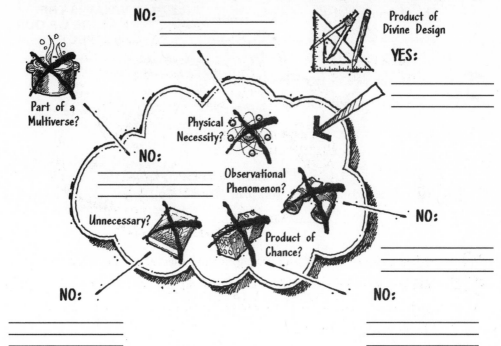

"Inside the Room" or "Outside the Room"
The Weakness of Internal Explanations Compared to the Strength of External Explanations

NO: _____

Product of Divine Design

YES: _____

Part of a Multiverse?

NO: _____

Physical Necessity?

Observational Phenomenon?

NO: _____

Unnecessary?

Product of Chance?

NO: _____

NO: _____

FORM A STRATEGIC PLAN
(5 MINUTES – EXAMINE YOUR CALENDAR AND CREATE AN ACTION PLAN)

Set aside time this week (schedule it on your calendar) to read the following biblical passages:

Genesis 1:1–2

Psalm 33:6

Psalm 90:2

Psalm 121:1–2

Jeremiah 32:17

Ephesians 2:10

Choose someone you know who would benefit from what you've learned about the fine-tuning of the universe: _____

_____

 Select a passage or two from the above list to share with this friend: _____

_____

_____

Set a date and time when you plan on sharing: _____

Our Emerging "Suspect" Profile:

WHAT IS THE NATURE OF OUR "SUSPECT"?

Given what we know so far, the cause of the universe is:

   1. external to the universe

   2. nonspatial, atemporal, and nonmaterial

   3. uncaused

   4. powerful enough to create everything we see in the universe

   5. specifically purposeful enough to produce a universe fine-tuned for life

 ## MAKE A CLOSING STATEMENT
(1 MINUTE – CONTEMPLATE AND PRAY)

The fine-tuning we observe in the universe is not the product of chance, necessity, or observational phenomena. God remains the most reasonable explanation for the fine-tuning of the cosmos. Our "suspect" profile is starting to take shape, as we see how the fine-tuning of the universe implies intentionality and purpose.

 Dear Lord, the deep concern You have for our well-being is displayed in the minute details required for life on our planet. The conditions of the universe are precisely and perfectly tuned for the existence of life. The foundational laws of physics, regional properties of our solar system, and locational conditions of our planet are all fine-tuned to sustain us. We turn our grateful hearts and minds toward You in thanksgiving that You care about each and every person and about the details of our lives. In Jesus's name we pray, amen.

CONDUCT A SECONDARY INVESTIGATION
(READ ON YOUR OWN FOR BETTER UNDERSTANDING)

To better understand the issues raised in this session, read *God's Crime Scene* chapter 2, "Tampering with the Evidence: Who Is Responsible?" For an in-depth discussion of all the alternative scientific theories, read the Secondary Investigation section of *God's Crime Scene*, taking notes specifically on chapter 2 (pages 213–20).

_____

_____

_____

_____

_____

_____

_____

_____

_____

_____

_____

_____

_____

_____

_____

Session Three
THE ORIGIN OF LIFE
Does the Text Require an Author?

Ethan Carmichael was brutally stabbed to death in the workshop of his large electronics store on the evening of December 30. Our team stood around Ethan's body, careful not to step in his blood or displace any evidence, including the cell phone lying near his right leg. I was the last person to arrive at the scene, and the first responding officers told me a woman had discovered Ethan's body. Her name was Rachel and she was Ethan's live-in girlfriend of several years.

I was particularly interested in Ethan's cell phone. When CSI finished their work, I searched through its data for relevant information. I discovered an interesting text, sent earlier in the evening. The short message was simply:

Bti30

The text appeared to come from a local phone number, but Ethan hadn't assigned a name to the number in his phone. What did the text mean? Was this *information* of some sort, or just chance gibberish? Where did it come from? Did someone intentionally text this string of characters, or was it transmitted accidentally? At first glance, it was nearly impossible to answer these questions, but within twenty-four hours I knew precisely what the message meant, where it came from, and who sent it.

We wrote a search warrant for Ethan's computer, phone, and business records, and I spent the better part of the next day combing through the results. First, I discovered the phone number was Rachel's newly activated cell phone. As I sifted through Ethan's cell phone texts and computer emails, I also discovered additional "Bti30" texts. Rachel and

Ethan regularly used this terminology when referring to their arrival times with each other. "Bti30" was simply shorthand for "Be there in 30 minutes."

As it turned out, Rachel and Ethan had been fighting for several months. Rachel had been seeing another man, Billy, during this time and had promised Billy she'd break up with Ethan prior to the year's end. On the night of the murder, Ethan was working late. When he was finally ready to go home, he received a text from Rachel indicating she would meet him at the business in thirty minutes. He stayed and was killed within the hour. Rachel then arrived nearly ninety minutes after the text and reportedly discovered Ethan's body.

We ultimately determined Rachel sent the text message for a distinct purpose. She wanted to delay Ethan's departure from the office just long enough for Billy to make it to the location and commit the murder. Rachel used a short burst of *information* to accomplish her murderous goal. *Information* within the crime scene pointed to an *external* suspect.

Information solved our homicide case, and in a similar way, *information* can help us investigate another piece of evidence in the cosmos as we try to answer the question: "How did life originate in the universe?" The building blocks of life in our universe (proteins, ribosomes, enzymes, and other cellular building blocks) are formed at the direction of *DNA*, the largest molecule known to scientists. The nucleotides in DNA molecules are ordered in a complex, *specified* manner. DNA contains *information* that has meaning and purpose. From where can this kind of information come? Can space, time, matter, physics, or chemistry cause information like the kind we see in DNA? Can we stay *inside* the "room" of the natural universe for an explanation, or is the existence of an "intruder" a better explanation?

Cold-Case Approach:

HOW CAN WE USE WHAT, WHERE, WHY, WHEN, AND HOW QUESTIONS TO DISCOVER WHO IS RESPONSIBLE?

In order to determine who committed a crime, we often begin by asking the classic "five Ws and one H" questions formulated by the ancient Greek thinker Hermagoras and popularized by Rudyard Kipling in *Just So Stories*.

This well-vetted approach to information gathering may not always provide us with the identity of the suspect, but it can usually help us eliminate unreasonable alternatives.

In this session, we'll ask these classic questions to identify important characteristics of our "suspect."

In this session, we'll examine the appearance of life in the universe as we seek to answer these important questions.

OPEN THE CASE FILE

(4 MINUTES – CONSIDER AND ANSWER AS MANY QUESTIONS AS POSSIBLE)

All of us write messages to friends and family members. Sometimes these messages are incredibly brief. Think about the last time you wrote a short message (either a very brief note, a text message, or social media message). If you have access to that message, write it here:

_____

_____

_____

What made this message understandable to the person who read it? Why did the receiver of this message know that it contained *information* rather than *gibberish*?

_____

_____

_____

Examine the following common abbreviations and write out as many of their meanings as you can:

ASAP _____

LOL _____

DIY _____

ROFL _____

ETA _____

Why are we able to decipher abbreviated "codes" such as these? Why do we believe that these abbreviations contain *information*?

_____

_____

_____

VIEW THE VIDEO TESTIMONY
(13 MINUTES – TAKE NOTES)

Asking good questions about biology: "What?" and "Where?"

_____

_____

_____

Asking good questions about biology: "Why?" and "When?"

_____

_____

_____

Investigating DNA

_____

_____

_____

Examining the five levels of information

_____

    Example 1: *ljp?fgn ksdnm, ni3shdo bfist, tt tt tt tt tt tt*

_____

Example 2: *grand the, eats letting*

_____

Example 3: *Grandpa is eating*

_____

Example 4: *Let's eat, Grandpa*

_____

Let's eat, Grandpa!

Let's eat Grandpa!

Applying information theory to DNA

_____
_____
_____

Asking a missing question: "Who?"

_____
_____
_____

CONDUCT A GROUP INVESTIGATION
(23 MINUTES – INVESTIGATE THE ISSUES AND ANSWER THE QUESTIONS)

Read the following paragraphs and questions aloud, then work together to provide answers.

J. Warner referred to the complexity of organic life in the video; here is just one example. The ordered, informational nucleotides in DNA are difficult to explain without divine guidance. Why? Because nucleotide bases display "homochirality" (single-handedness). Just as you and I have two hands (one right and one left), nucleotide bases, sugars, amino acids, and other "life-necessary" molecules demonstrate similar "handedness."

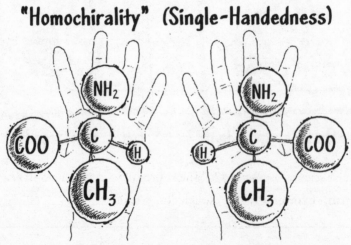

"Homochirality" (Single-Handedness)

"Left-Handed" Amino Acid   "Right-Handed" Amino Acid

Proteins cannot assemble unless their "chiral" amino acids are entirely "right- or left-handed"

Scientists trying to explain the origin of life from *inside* the "room" of the natural universe *cannot* answer a critical question: How did the single-handed nucleotides, sugars, and amino acids develop from a "primordial soup" that was both left- *and* right-handed? When chemists perform tests to duplicate the creation of these critical organic molecules—without intervening as an intelligent agent—they emerge in an almost *equal* mixture of left- and right-handed molecules.

 Why do you think homochirality presents a problem for those who deny the existence of God?

_____

_____

_____

Scientists who try to explain the informational nature of the nucleotide order in DNA—while denying the existence of a Divine Author—have offered two responses. Examine both responses (referring to your notes from this session's video), and work in unison to answer the following questions.

 Secular scientist response #1: "DNA is not really information." Explain why this explanation is faulty:

_____

_____

_____

 Secular scientist response #2: "The laws of physics and chemistry can create information." Explain why this explanation is faulty:

_____

_____

_____

Read John 1:1–3:

In the beginning was the Word, and the Word was with God, and the Word was God. He was in the beginning with God. All things came into being through Him, and apart from Him nothing came into being that has come into being.

What does this tell us about Jesus? Is Jesus a created being? What activity is attributed to Jesus in these verses?

_____

_____

_____

 Read Hebrews 12:2:

Fixing our eyes on Jesus, the author and perfecter of faith, who for the joy set before Him endured the cross, despising the shame, and has sat down at the right hand of the throne of God.

This verse describes Jesus as the "author and perfecter" of our faith. While it describes Jesus's role in our salvation (our life with *God*), how might this descriptor apply to His role in creating our life in the *universe*?

_____

_____

_____

Read the box to the right, which provides a "Tool for the Call-Out Bag." Use your notes to fill in the different levels of information J. Warner spoke about in the session video.

A Tool for the Call-Out Bag:

CAN DEGREES OF INFORMATION TELL US SOMETHING ABOUT THE IDENTITY OF A SUSPECT?

J. Warner described the work of Dr. Werner Gitt, who provided the following helpful distinctions related to the nature of information (and its relationship to intelligent suspects):

LEVEL 1—_____: a quantity and sequence of symbols devoid of obvious origin or meaning

LEVEL 2—_____: symbol combinations (words) derived from an agreed-upon set of rules yet still devoid of assembled meaning

LEVEL 3—_____: symbols, words, phrases, and sentences possessing meaning understood by both the sender and receiver

LEVEL 4—_____: symbols, words, phrases, and sentences directing a specific action (requested by the sender and expected of the receiver)

LEVEL 5—_____: the intended goal or purpose of the sender as he or she is using symbols, words, phrases, and sentences to accomplish a specific outcome

Which level of information is possible from *inside* the "room" of the natural universe using simply physics and chemistry?

_____

Which level of information most closely approximates the kind of information we find in DNA?

_____

 TAKE A PERSONAL ASSESSMENT
(4 MINUTES – EXAMINE YOUR OWN SITUATION AND ANSWER THE QUESTIONS)

In this session we've asked classic investigative questions in an effort to identify where, when, why, and how life originated. Much of this scientific information may seem unfamiliar or largely forgotten to you (even if you studied it in school). Be honest about your level of readiness related to scientific matters.

 How would you rate yourself on a scale of 1 to 10, 1 being "unprepared to discuss scientific matters" and 10 being "equipped and ready to talk about science and biology"? _____

 How can you better prepare yourself to discuss the improbability of biological life emerging from inorganic matter in the universe? What books might you read? What subjects could you study, either online or at the library?

_____

_____

_____

Look at the following diagram illustrating the investigative questions related to the origin of life:

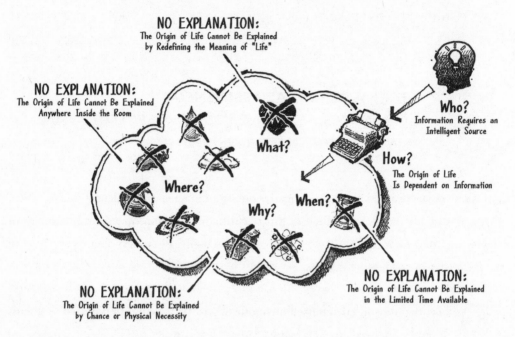

"Inside the Room" or "Outside the Room"
The Weakness of Internal Explanations Compared to the Strength of External Explanations

NO EXPLANATION:
The Origin of Life Cannot Be Explained by Redefining the Meaning of "Life"

NO EXPLANATION:
The Origin of Life Cannot Be Explained Anywhere Inside the Room

What?

Where?

Why?   When?

Who?
Information Requires an Intelligent Source

How?
The Origin of Life Is Dependent on Information

NO EXPLANATION:
The Origin of Life Cannot Be Explained by Chance or Physical Necessity

NO EXPLANATION:
The Origin of Life Cannot Be Explained in the Limited Time Available

Based on what you've learned so far, formulate a response you might give to someone who thinks science shouldn't be allowed to ask a "who" question:

_____

_____

_____

Now go take the additional step and formulate how you might make the case (based on the diagram above) for a Divine Author of the information found in DNA:

_____

_____

_____

FORM A STRATEGIC PLAN
(5 MINUTES – EXAMINE YOUR CALENDAR AND CREATE AN ACTION PLAN)

There is likely someone in your life who might resonate with the evidence found in DNA. Take a moment to identify one or two people you know who are fascinated with science and convinced that scientific disciplines can explain our existence. Set a date to talk with them to share the truth about the information in DNA:

Identify the person(s) with whom you want to share:

_____

Set a date(s) to share:

_____

As you share the truth about the information in DNA (and God as the best inference as its author), be prepared to share what the Bible says about how God has also authored *Scripture*. Take the time to bookmark or memorize the verses you might share.

Set a date to read the following verses in one setting:

_____

Summarize the most memorable and powerful takeaways you had from each verse in the space provided:

Psalm 12:6

_____

Proverbs 30:5

_____

Matthew 4:4

_____

2 Timothy 3:16–17

_____

Hebrews 4:12

_____

MAKE A CLOSING STATEMENT
(1 MINUTE – CONTEMPLATE AND PRAY)

Our "suspect profile" looks more and more like the God of the Bible, and our inference isn't based simply on the lack of naturalistic explanations *inside* the "room," but is instead an inference from the *affirmative* evidence we've described in DNA. Information comes only from *intelligence*; physics and chemistry cannot account for what we find in DNA. The best explanation for this information is an intelligent source *outside* of space, time, and matter.

Our Emerging "Suspect" Profile:

WHAT IS THE NATURE OF OUR "SUSPECT"?

Given what we know so far, the cause of the universe is:

1. External to the universe

2. Nonspatial, atemporal, and nonmaterial

3. Uncaused

4. Powerful enough to create everything we see in the universe

5. Specifically purposeful enough to produce a universe fine-tuned for life

6. Intelligent and communicative

Dear God, the famous hymn "How Great Thou Art," written by Carl Boberg, makes clear the splendor of Your Being. We are in awesome wonder when we consider all that You have powerfully created. From the enormous stars and planets to humans, plants, and animals, to the detailed information in DNA, Your intelligence is evident. Our souls sing praises as You allow us to discover and learn more about You through Your creation. Please help us to notice the

glory of Your creation every day and remind us of the intelligence from which
it came into existence. We pray this in Jesus's name, amen.

CONDUCT A SECONDARY INVESTIGATION
(READ ON YOUR OWN FOR BETTER UNDERSTANDING)

The information in this session has been taken from *God's Crime Scene* chapter 3, "The Origin of Life: Does the Text Require an Author?" For an in-depth discussion of why an intelligent cause *outside* the "room" of the natural universe is the best inference from evidence, read the Secondary Investigation section of *God's Crime Scene*, taking notes specifically on chapter 3 (pages 220–27).

_____

_____

_____

_____

_____

_____

_____

_____

_____

_____

_____

_____

_____

_____

Session Four
SIGNS OF DESIGN
Is There Evidence of an Artist?

Officers Ed Timmons and Randy Campbell arrived at the scene in the middle of the night. A resident, Angela Harvey, called the police to report a possible murder, and as soon as Ed and Randy made it to the location, she ran from the front door, waving her arms in the air.

"Hurry! Something's happened to Linda!" Angela pointed to the rear unit of her duplex. "I heard screaming and there's blood everywhere!"

Ed and Randy followed Angela to Linda's residence. Linda's front door was ajar, and Randy observed blood smears on the doorknob. He used his baton to push open the door. Linda's apartment was small and dark. A chair in the entryway was overturned, and bloody footsteps led back to the rear bedroom. Ed followed the trail down a short hall, where a small potted ficus tree was lying on its side. On the ground, next to the potted tree, lay a twisted wire. Randy knew what it was the moment he saw it, even though it was covered in blood.

Linda Seymour was lying on her bed. She had clearly been in a struggle. Her throat was deeply severed; her lifeless body was covered in blood. Ed removed the portable radio from his belt and asked the dispatcher for a supervisor. Detectives were later called and arrived on the scene within forty minutes.

Randy guided the investigators to the wire murder weapon lying next to the ficus. Detective Paul Rigdon was new to the investigative team at the time, and like most homicide detectives, he'd never seen a garrote in person. He recognized it, however, because he had recently watched the newly released film *The Godfather*. Four characters in Coppola's film were killed with a garrote, and Rigdon immediately recognized the design features of the simple weapon.

A thin wire (approximately eighteen inches long) was lying next to the potted tree. It might easily have been mistaken for the wire used to tie the ficus to its support stick, but this particular wire was attached at each end to two five-inch-long wooden dowels. Each dowel had a small hole drilled at its center, through which the wire was threaded and tied carefully with a knot.

The garrote was collected from the interior of the crime scene on the night of the murder. It was a pivotal piece of evidence; the weapon had been *designed* for a purpose and reflected the character and expertise of its *designer*.

When we say something is "designed," we mean it was created intentionally and planned for a purpose. Designed objects are fashioned by intelligent agents who have a goal in mind, and their creations reflect the purpose for which they were created.

The moment Randy Campbell and Paul Rigdon observed the garrote, they knew it wasn't simply a piece of wire and wood dislodged from the ficus pot. Why? Because it possessed several characteristics reasonably associated with *designed* objects. In a similar way, scientists (including *atheist* scientists like Richard Dawkins) recognize design features in biological organisms in our universe. Dawkins even described the field of biology as "the study of complicated things that give the appearance of having been designed for a purpose."[1] In this session, we'll identify the common characteristics of design and examine the nature of biological organisms in an effort to answer the question: "Does the appearance of biological design *inside* the 'room' of the natural universe point to the existence of a Designer *outside* the 'room'?"

Cold-Case Approach:

HOW DO WE ASSEMBLE CUMULATIVE, CIRCUMSTANTIAL CASES TO ARRIVE AT REASONABLE INFERENCES?

Sometimes I'm lucky enough to have an eyewitness who can tell me what happened (direct evidence), but more often than not, I have to rely on a large collection of indirect (circumstantial) pieces of evidence to make my case.

In California, judges instruct jurors: "Both direct and circumstantial evidence are acceptable types of evidence to prove or disprove the elements of a charge, including intent and mental state and acts necessary to a conviction, and neither is necessarily more reliable than the other. Neither is entitled to any greater weight than the other."

In this session, we'll examine eight forms of circumstantial evidence pointing to a reasonable design inference.

OPEN THE CASE FILE
(5 MINUTES – CONSIDER AND ANSWER AS MANY QUESTIONS AS POSSIBLE)

1. Examine the pen or pencil you are using to write in this participant's guide. If someone claimed it came into existence without a pen or pencil *designer*, what would you say?

_____

_____

_____

2. Do your best to list three or four attributes of the pen or pencil that demonstrate it has been designed by an intelligent designer:

Attribute: *Why this attribute requires a designer:*

_____   _____

                     _____

_____   _____

                     _____

_____   _____

                     _____

_____   _____

                     _____

3. Now review the design attributes you've offered. If you were to read these attributes to someone *without* identifying the object, would they recognize you were describing a pen or pencil? _____ Why does the appearance of design always tell us something about the *purpose* of the designed object?

_____

_____

_____

VIEW THE VIDEO TESTIMONY
(13 MINUTES - TAKE NOTES AND FILL IN THE DIAGRAM)

Identifying the attributes of design at a crime scene

_____

_____

_____

Describing the attributes of design (in a garotte)

Dubious Probability (Chance)

_____

_____

Echoes of Familiarity (Pattern)

_____

_____

Sophistication and Intricacy

_____

_____

Informational Dependency

_____

_____

Goal Direction (and Intentionality)

_____

_____

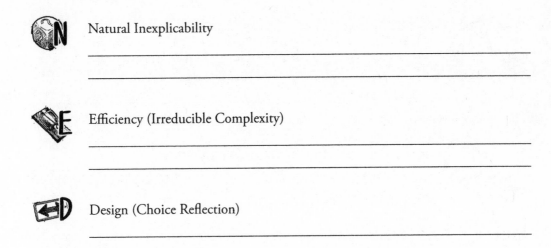

Natural Inexplicability

_____

_____

Efficiency (Irreducible Complexity)

_____

_____

Design (Choice Reflection)

_____

_____

Identifying the attributes of design in a bacterial flagellum

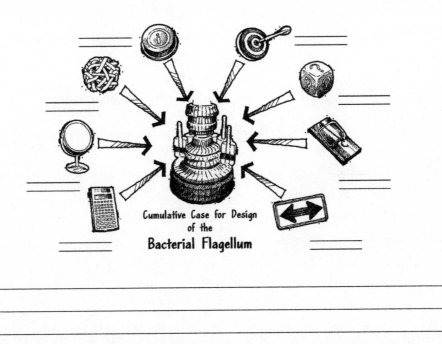

Cumulative Case for Design
of the
Bacterial Flagellum

_____

_____

_____

_____

Examining an evolutionary explanation for bacterial flagellum

_____

_____

_____

CONDUCT A GROUP INVESTIGATION

(22 MINUTES – INVESTIGATE THE ISSUES AND ANSWER THE QUESTIONS)

Read aloud the following paragraphs related to the "appearance" of design in biology (from _God's Crime Scene_), then answer the related questions:

As unlikely and unexpected as it may be, life exists in our universe, and just as researchers stipulate to the appearance of fine-tuning in the cosmos, scientists also stipulate to the appearance of design in biological organisms.

Many other scientists affirm this observation and extend it to include the larger ecosystems in which many symbiotic organisms are dependent on one another for their survival. Smith College professor of biological sciences Robert Dorit said, "The apparent fit between organisms seems to suggest some higher intelligence at work, some supervisory gardener bringing harmony and color to the garden."[2] For scientists looking for an explanation within the "garden" to avoid the inference of an external "supervisory gardener," this appearance of design is difficult to explain.

A Tool for the Call-Out Bag:

HOW CAN WE MAKE REASONABLE INFERENCES TO FORM SENSIBLE EXPLANATIONS?

Detectives draw conclusions from evidence. Some inferences from evidence are more reasonable than others. In legal terms, an inference is a "deduction of fact that may logically and _reasonably_ be drawn from another fact or group of facts found or otherwise established" (Cal. Code evid: 600 [b]).

Reasonable inferences are "conclusions which are regarded as logical by reasonable people in the light of their experience in life" (Lannon v. Hogan, 719 F.2d 518, 521 [1st Cir. Mass. 1983]). Because each of us has experience with designed objects, we are sufficiently capable of inferring design when we see it.

1. Why do you think atheist scientists reject the possibility (let alone reasonable inference) of a Designer to explain what they call the "appearance" of design?

_____

_____

_____

2. Review the diagram of the bacterial flagellum motor. Which of the attributes of design do you think is most difficult to explain without the intervention of a Designer?

Attribute: *Why the attribute is difficult to explain:*

_____   _____

_____   _____

Read the following passage (paraphrased from *God's Crime Scene*) aloud, then work together to answer the questions:

The design of my duty weapon, a Glock 21 pistol, reflects more than creativity; it reflects purpose ... The individual parts are assembled carefully and sequentially for a specific reason to achieve a specific objective. When I disassemble the Glock for cleaning, I must do it in a particular order: squeezing the trigger, pulling back the slide slightly, pushing down the take-down levers, removing the slide barrel assembly, pushing and releasing the recoil spring, and finally removing the barrel assembly. After cleaning, the gun must be reassembled in reverse order. The gun's designer clearly created an assembly pathway allowing for the initial construction of the gun (and I can discover this pathway by trying to successfully deconstruct the pistol). This pathway is intentional and purposeful; it achieves its goal.

Now compare the assembly sequence of the pistol to the assembly sequence of bacterial flagellum:

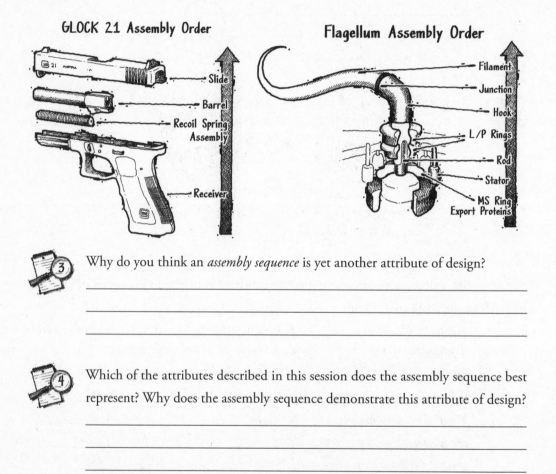

GLOCK 21 Assembly Order

- Slide
- Barrel
- Recoil Spring Assembly
- Receiver

Flagellum Assembly Order

- Filament
- Junction
- Hook
- L/P Rings
- Rod
- Stator
- MS Ring
- Export Proteins

3 Why do you think an *assembly sequence* is yet another attribute of design?

_____

_____

_____

4 Which of the attributes described in this session does the assembly sequence best represent? Why does the assembly sequence demonstrate this attribute of design?

_____

_____

_____

Atheist scientists believe the complex flagellum was formed through an evolutionary process by *borrowing* from a less complex biological "machine" called a "type III secretion system" (as J. Warner described in the video). They believe the "T3SS" was modified by evolutionary processes until the flagellum emerged:

The Irreducibly Complex
**Type Three Secretion
System (T3SS)**

The Irreducibly Complex
**Bacterial Flagellum
Motor**

 There are several problems with this explanation for bacterial flagellum. Examine each problematic truth related to type three secretion systems, then describe why this truth would eliminate the possibility that the secretion system evolved into the flagellum:

Problematic T3SS truth: Reason this eliminates evolution as an explanation:

The T3SS is irreducibly _____

complex to 30 proteins _____

_____

_____

The T3SS is now believed _____

to be YOUNGER than the _____

flagellum _____

_____

TAKE A PERSONAL ASSESSMENT

(4 MINUTES – EXAMINE YOUR OWN SITUATION AND ANSWER THE QUESTIONS)

Examine the emerging "suspect" profile to the right. Fill in the additional "suspect" characteristic(s), given the evidence from the appearance of design.

Designed objects are created for a purpose. What does the design (fine-tuning) of the universe *and* the design of humans tell us about God's overarching purpose in history?

_____

_____

_____

Our Emerging "Suspect" Profile:

WHAT IS THE NATURE OF OUR "SUSPECT"?

Given what we know so far, the cause of the universe is:

1. external to the universe

2. nonspatial, atemporal, and nonmaterial

3. uncaused

4. powerful enough to create everything we see in the universe

5. specifically purposeful enough to produce a universe fine-tuned for life

6. intelligent and communicative

7. _____

_____

Read Job 10:9–12:

Remember now, that You have made me as clay; and would You turn me into dust again? Did You not pour me out like milk and curdle me like cheese; clothe me with skin and flesh, and _____ with bones and sinews? You have granted me life and lovingkindness; and Your care has preserved my spirit.

According to this verse, God has designed each of us with loving-kindness and His care has preserved our spirits. Lovingly designed objects are created for a *purpose*.

 Use the following prompts to think about God's purpose for your life.

My God-given gifts: _____

_____

_____

My interests and passions: _____

_____

_____

My location and situation: _____

_____

_____

What purpose do you think God has for you, given that He designed you with these gifts and desires and placed you in the context you presently experience?

_____

_____

_____

FORM A STRATEGIC PLAN
(5 MINUTES – EXAMINE YOUR CALENDAR AND CREATE AN ACTION PLAN)

Read 1 Peter 2:9:

But you are a chosen race, a royal priesthood, a holy nation, a people for God's own possession, so that you may proclaim the excellencies of Him who has called you out of darkness into His marvelous light.

Given this description of God's purpose for our lives, how might you (based on your gifts, passions, and situation) "proclaim the excellencies of Him who has called you"? Provide three practical ways you can fulfill your purpose over the next year.

1. _____

    _____

2. _____

    _____

3. _____

    _____

 Imagine sharing the evidence from design with someone in your life. Who do you think God has prepared for a conversation such as this? _____

_____

When will you have this conversation? _____

 MAKE A CLOSING STATEMENT
(1 MINUTE – CONTEMPLATE AND PRAY)

When we observe the cumulative, circumstantial case for design in biological systems, it's reasonable to infer an intelligent designer, and this designer has demonstrated a degree of ingenuity and creativity unparalleled by human standards. The evidence of design in biology provides even more information about the external cause of the universe. Our suspect is powerful, intelligent, and creative. What kind of external suspect could fit our growing list of characteristics? As we are about to see in the next session, the best explanation for the creative cause of the universe is a *mind*.

Dear God, based on what we know about the nature of design and given the cumulative appearance of many design attributes, we can reasonably conclude that You, our Intelligent Designer, created us with a purpose in mind. Thank You for the gifts of creativity You have placed within each of us. We rejoice in these gifts because we know they are evidence of our being made in Your image. Help us to proclaim your "excellencies" to the world around us. In Your precious Son's name we pray, amen.

CONDUCT A SECONDARY INVESTIGATION
(READ ON YOUR OWN FOR BETTER UNDERSTANDING)

Examine the following diagram from *God's Crime Scene*. It summarizes the weakness of explanations people offer from *inside* the "room" of the universe when trying to describe the appearance of design in biology.

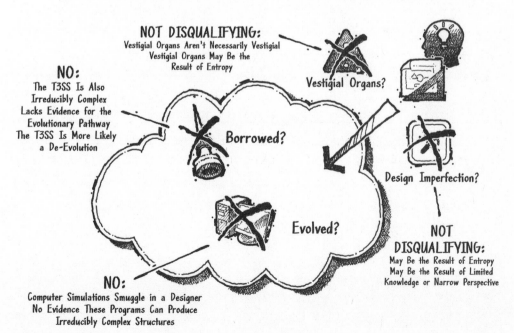

"Inside the Room" or "Outside the Room"
The Weakness of Internal Explanations Compared to the Strength of External Explanations

NOT DISQUALIFYING:
Vestigial Organs Aren't Necessarily Vestigial
Vestigial Organs May Be the Result of Entropy

Vestigial Organs?

NO:
The T3SS Is Also Irreducibly Complex
Lacks Evidence for the Evolutionary Pathway
The T3SS Is More Likely a De-Evolution

Borrowed?

Design Imperfection?

Evolved?

NOT DISQUALIFYING:
May Be the Result of Entropy
May Be the Result of Limited Knowledge or Narrow Perspective

NO:
Computer Simulations Smuggle in a Designer
No Evidence These Programs Can Produce Irreducibly Complex Structures

You'll notice that this diagram also describes two objections that are leveled against the existence of an Intelligent Designer (the existence of vestigial organs, and the claim of design imperfection). For an in-depth discussion of why an intelligent cause *outside* the "room" of the natural universe is the best inference from evidence (in spite of these objections), read the Secondary Investigation section of *God's Crime Scene*, taking notes specifically on chapter 4, "Signs of Design: Is There Evidence of an Artist?" (pages 227–39).

_____

_____

_____

_____

_____

_____

_____

_____

_____

_____

_____

_____

_____

Session Five

OUR EXPERIENCE OF CONSCIOUSNESS

Are We More Than Matter?

I was the first detective to arrive at the murder scene. The front door was ajar, and I could see Ryan Gelder's lifeless body in the entry hall of the modest house. Ryan was six years old and today was his birthday. His father, Ted Gelder, shot Ryan after murdering Ryan's grandmother and shooting Ryan's mother, Teresa, in the arm. Ted then shot himself. The murder-suicide claimed four victims.

Ted was estranged from Teresa and upset he wasn't allowed to see Ryan on his birthday. Ted blamed Teresa for the state of their marriage and the miserable nature of his own life following their separation.

As the other detectives and investigative personnel arrived at the murder scene, I prepared myself for their reactions. I knew the case would be difficult for some of them. It's not every day you see a victim this young murdered in such a brutal way—and by his own father. I observed three separate reactions from the investigators who stood over Ryan's body.

One of them, Cynthia Moulton, was a relatively new officer, recently assigned to the crime scene investigation detail. It was her responsibility to photograph the scene and carefully collect the pertinent pieces of physical evidence. She had a five-year-old boy of her own and reacted emotionally the moment she saw Ryan. Though she did her best to perform her duties, eventually she retreated from the house and told her sergeant to call for a replacement.

As Cynthia walked back to her CSI vehicle, many of the older detectives dealt with their discomfort by jesting about Ted's accuracy (given the small target Ryan presented). Some made awkward, inappropriate jokes while standing beside the murder victims. I'd seen this kind of reaction at other murder scenes; for many people, dark humor of this nature is a survival mechanism. Those who take these scenes too seriously will ultimately drive themselves crazy; those who learn to brush them aside with some form of humor—even inappropriately dark humor—typically do better. I wasn't comfortable with either approach.

As someone who believed in the existence of God, I embraced a third response, grounded in my conclusions as a Christian. I rejected the idea Ryan's life had been terminated completely by his father. If, as humans, we are nothing more than physical bodies and brains, Ryan's murder necessitated the kind of coping response I observed: some who grieve, some who joke. If, on the other hand, we are more than purely physical creatures—a combination of brain and *mind*, body, and *soul*—we might respond to Ryan's *physical* death differently. If we recognize the difference between the material and *nonmaterial* Ryan, there are good reasons to be confident Ryan, as a *nonmaterial soul*, is still alive.

Cold-Case Approach:

WHAT IS ABDUCTIVE REASONING?

Detectives use *abductive reasoning* to arrive at the most reasonable explanation (or suspect) in a case. This form of reasoning requires investigators to consider cumulative collections of evidence as they compare competing explanations to determine which, if any, of these explanations is reasonable. Explanations are evaluated on the basis of their feasibility, their ability to account for all the evidence offered, their straightforward simplicity, and their logical consistency.

In this session, we'll employ abductive reasoning to determine which inference is most reasonable in explaining the existence and nature of the *mind*.

The nonphysical identity of Ryan, if it truly exists, is impossible to explain from within the physical limits of the material universe. If we stay in the "room" of the universe to create Ryan from scratch, the only ingredients available to us are matter, space, and time. The only instruments available are the laws of physics and chemistry and the steady influence of environmental conditions.

But Ryan (and the rest of us) seem to be more than simply material beings. We have material brains, but we also experience *nonmaterial minds*. In this session, we'll examine the nature of consciousness and the existence of mind to see if the best explanation lies *outside* the "room" of the material universe.

OPEN THE CASE FILE

(5 MINUTES – CONSIDER AND ANSWER AS MANY QUESTIONS AS POSSIBLE)

Read Romans 12:2:

> *And do not be conformed to this world, but be transformed by the renewing of your mind, so that you may prove what the will of God is, that which is good and acceptable and perfect.*

What role does your mind (your thought life) play in aiding your Christian transformation?

_____

_____

_____

The Christian worldview describes several immaterial (nonphysical) realities and beings, including minds, souls, angels, and demons. Angels and humans are created beings. List the ways in which these two created beings are different:

Humans: Angelic Beings:

_____   _____

_____   _____

_____   _____

_____   _____

_____   _____

Your body is different from your soul. List some of the differences:

Body: Soul:

_____   _____

_____   _____

_____   _____

_____   _____

_____   _____

_____   _____

VIEW THE VIDEO TESTIMONY
(12 MINUTES – TAKE NOTES)

Examining the "law of identity" and the difference between "brain" and "mind"

_____

_____

_____

Examining the distinction between "public" and "private"

_____

_____

_____

Investigating the distinction between "is-ness" and "about-ness" (intentionality)

_____

_____

_____

Studying the distinction between "incorrect" and "indisputable"

_____

_____

_____

Exploring the distinction between "impersonal" and "personal"

_____

_____

_____

Considering the distinction between "measurable" and "immeasurable"

_____

_____

_____

Accounting for consciousness from *inside* the "room" of the universe: "behaviorism"

_____

_____

_____

 **CONDUCT A GROUP INVESTIGATION**
(23 MINUTES – INVESTIGATE THE ISSUES AND ANSWER THE QUESTIONS)

As you read this paragraph, you're probably aware of your own thoughts related to its contents—your feelings, sensations, ideas, and desires resulting from what you've read so far. You are having a *conscious* experience. Consciousness poses one of the most difficult conundrums for philosophers and scientists. As atheist philosopher (and cognitive scientist)

David Chalmers lamented, "Conscious experience is at once the most familiar thing in the world and the most mysterious. There is nothing we know about more directly than consciousness, but it is far from clear how to reconcile it with everything else we know. Why does it exist? What does it do? How could it possibly arise from lumpy gray matter?"[1]

In the video, J. Warner described one way philosophers try to explain consciousness from *inside* the "room" of the universe (behaviorism). Read aloud the following paragraphs describing three additional ways philosophers try to explain consciousness as something *material*, then answer the related questions:

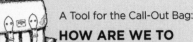

A Tool for the Call-Out Bag:

HOW ARE WE TO CONSIDER THE STRENGTHS AND WEAKNESSES OF EVIDENCE?

In all my years investigating and presenting criminal cases, I've learned an important truth: *Every* case (and *every* explanation) possesses both explanatory *liabilities* and explanatory *virtues*. Even the best explanations—those that happen to be true—typically possess evidential deficiencies of one kind or another.

But even though true explanations aren't always evidentially perfect, they usually possess far fewer liabilities than the alternative explanations. When examining any set of accounts, we must always recognize the ratio of liabilities to virtues.

When an explanation suffers from more deficiencies than assets, it's reasonable to favor the explanation with fewer liabilities.

Are Mental States Merely Brain States?

Some scientists and philosophers believe the brain and the mind are one and the same. According to this approach, mental states such as anger or pain are identical to brain states; they are nothing more than physical, material, neurological activities in the brain.

1. In the video, J. Warner described the many ways the *brain* is different from the *mind*. Why do these differences disqualify this explanation for consciousness?

_____

_____

_____

2. Physical brains are subject to the laws of *physics*; mental states are subject to the laws of *logic*. If your thoughts are simply the result of *physical processes*, what

difficulty would this present? Why would this cause us to doubt we are thinking *freely* for ourselves?

_____

_____

_____

Are Mental States Only Functional States?

Some philosophers prefer to see the mind as a complex machine of sorts. This is called *machine-state functionalism*. According to this view, our brains are physical machines programmed with instructions and capable of receiving sensory input like physical computers.

Even if computers sometimes produce specific responses with the *appearance* of understanding, do you think they have *true* understanding? Why, or why not?

_____

_____

_____

Every Windows- or Apple-based operating system processes input and provides output in the *same* way, based on the common operating systems. While humans have a common physical "operating system"—the brain—we don't share common thoughts, feelings, or responses to stimuli. Why do you think humans respond differently, and how does this fact eliminate *machine-state functionalism* as an explanation of consciousness?

_____

_____

_____

Are Mental States Nonexistent?

According to *eliminative materialism*, when we try to describe the activity in the physical brain, we simply use the outdated words "mental states." Eliminative materialists believe this language needs to be changed. By eliminating our antiquated descriptions of mental states, these philosophers hope to stay "inside the room" of the physical universe for an explanation of consciousness—by eliminating the notion of "mental states" altogether.

 Return to the "Tool for the Call-Out Bag" in session 1 describing bad explanations. Which of the three kinds of bad explanations does *eliminative materialism* sound like?

_____

 Eliminativists believe something is true *about* mental states: their *nonexistence*. Do you see the contradiction? Return to your notes from the video for this session related to the "is-ness" of the *brain* and the "about-ness" of the *mind*. How can eliminativists have a belief *about* something unless their mental states are something other than physical? Describe why the "about-ness" of their theory gives their theory away.

_____

_____

_____

TAKE A PERSONAL ASSESSMENT
(4 MINUTES – EXAMINE YOUR OWN SITUATION AND ANSWER THE QUESTIONS)

Theories of consciousness are sometimes difficult to understand. Which of the theories offered by people trying to stay inside the "room" of the universe has been the most difficult to grasp, and why?

_____

_____

_____

 Imagine trying to briefly explain why none of the theories for consciousness from *inside* the "room" of the universe adequately describe our experience of consciousness. Use the following diagram to organize your responses:

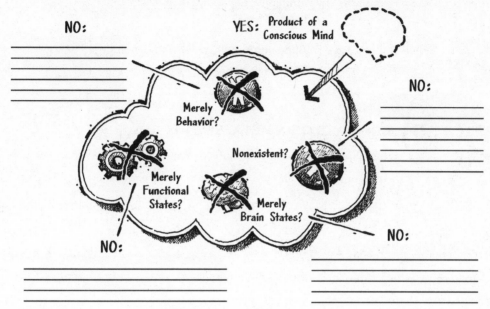

"Inside the Room" or "Outside the Room"
The Weakness of Internal Explanations Compared to the Strength of External Explanations

FORM A STRATEGIC PLAN
(5 MINUTES – EXAMINE YOUR CALENDAR AND CREATE AN ACTION PLAN)

Diagrams often help communicate difficult concepts. Refer to the prior diagram and attempt to draw your own version of it in the space below. You don't have to use the same icons for each explanation (you can make up your own), and you don't have to rewrite all your notes:

Imagine drawing this diagram quickly for someone with whom you are making the case for God. With whom would you share this information?

_____

When will you have an opportunity to share this information?

_____

MAKE A CLOSING STATEMENT
(1 MINUTE – CONTEMPLATE AND PRAY)

There are good reasons to conclude we are more than simply physical beings. We have brains *and* minds, bodies *and* souls. The case for the mind is strong; it is the most reasonable explanation for the phenomena we commonly experience as conscious creatures. But the mind cannot be explained from *inside* the "room." It forces us to look for a nonphysical, nonmaterial explanation *outside* the "room," beyond the material limits of the physical universe.

The existence of the nonmaterial *mind* is yet another piece of evidence pointing to a nonmaterial, *external* cause of the universe. Unlike the cosmological and biological evidences we've examined so far, this piece of evidence is wholly nonmaterial. It is part of a new category of evidences and adds an additional layer of complexity to our "suspect" profile.

Heavenly Father, thank You for our marvelous minds and our ability to think, reason, and make decisions. Our thoughts are our own and completely

Our Emerging "Suspect" Profile:

WHAT IS THE NATURE OF OUR "SUSPECT"?

Given what we know so far, the cause of the universe is:

1. external to the universe

2. nonspatial, atemporal, and nonmaterial

3. uncaused

4. powerful enough to create everything we see in the universe

5. specifically purposeful enough to produce a universe fine-tuned for life

6. intelligent and communicative

7. creative and resourceful

8. a conscious Mind

private. Only You, Lord, know our true thoughts and beliefs. The exclusively personal, subjective nature of mental states points to You as a personal God who is interested in our concerns, worries, fears, and hopes. Thank You for caring this deeply about us. Help us to trust You as You teach us through Your Word and guide us with Your Holy Spirit. In the name of Your Son, amen.

CONDUCT A SECONDARY INVESTIGATION
(READ ON YOUR OWN FOR BETTER UNDERSTANDING)

The information in this session has been taken from *God's Crime Scene* chapter 5, "Our Experience of Consciousness: Are We More Than Matter?" For an in-depth discussion of why an immaterial Mind *outside* the "room" of the natural universe is the best inference from evidence, read the Secondary Investigation section of *God's Crime Scene*, taking notes specifically on the objections leveled against the existence of immaterial consciousness (pages 239–50).

Objection: Immaterial Mental Interaction Is Difficult to Understand

_____

_____

_____

_____

Objection: The Immaterial Explanation Fails to Explain Examples Cited in Brain-Damaged Patients

_____

_____

_____

_____

Objection: The Immaterial Explanation Resists the Growing Acceptance of Physicalism

_____

_____

_____

_____

Objection: The Immaterial Explanation Is Simply the Result of Scientific Impatience

_____

_____

_____

_____

FREE WILL OR FULL WIRING

Are Real Choices Even Possible?

Paul Tonnegin and Sandy Holt looked weary and disheveled. Sandy parked her weathered Chevy Camaro in the nearly empty parking lot of a corner liquor store. Paul exited and started walking into the adjoining neighborhood. For a week prior, they had been getting high on heroin. Our surveillance team had been watching them for nearly two weeks after an informant told us Paul was responsible for a series of residential burglaries in our city. Now, eleven days into our surveillance, Paul and Sandy appeared to be out of money and out of dope.

Paul came from a *family* of heroin users. His father and brother had also been arrested for heroin possession, and his father was a convicted residential burglar. Today, many hours after shooting what little heroin he had left, Paul was coming down off his high, and like Sandy, he was starting to get sick. They needed money for heroin. Sandy drove into a nice neighborhood on the west side of our city, and Paul started looking for an opportunity.

Watching from unmarked vehicles, we saw Paul walk through the neighborhood carrying a backpack and knocking on several doors. If a resident answered, Paul said something to convince them he was there legitimately, then excused himself and continued down the street. At the fourth house he found his first unoccupied residence. When no one answered the door, he walked to the side yard and entered the backyard.

Members of our team, dressed in street clothes and carrying portable radios, scrambled to get into position. I contacted the residents to the rear of Paul's target house and asked for permission to enter their backyard. From over their fence I watched Paul as he peered into the windows of the victim's house. He tried the back door and found it to be locked.

Standing next to the door, Paul paused for a moment. Then, unexpectedly, he sat down on the porch, pulled out a cigarette, and began to smoke. I radioed my teammates and told them about Paul's actions. We wondered why he was hesitating. Minutes later, however, after finishing his cigarette, Paul stood up and kicked in the door. Our team tightened their position around the house. Paul eventually exited the front door with a full backpack and began to walk to Sandy's car. I jumped the fence and entered the victim's house. Paul had quickly ransacked the residence. I radioed this to the team and confirmed the burglary. Paul was arrested without incident about ten feet from Sandy's car.

Paul later told me he was tired of his life as an addict. He said he almost changed his mind about committing the burglary when he sat down on the porch. But he smoked the cigarette and gathered the courage to do the job. Given Paul's struggle as a drug addict, his upbringing in a family of criminals, and his hesitancy to complete the burglary, should he have been absolved of any responsibility in this crime? Did Paul choose to commit this crime *freely*, or was his behavior dictated by prior events outside of his control?

Cold-Case Approach:

HOW DO WE DETERMINE PERSONAL RESPONSIBILITY AND CRIMINAL INTENT?

Personal responsibility is assigned to every person who chooses to commit a crime when he or she could have chosen otherwise:

"A member of a conspiracy is criminally responsible for the crimes that he or she conspires to commit, no matter which member of the conspiracy commits the crime. A member of a conspiracy is also criminally responsible for any act of any member of the conspiracy if that act is done to further the conspiracy and that act is a natural and probable consequence of the common plan or design of the conspiracy.... Under this rule, a defendant who is a member of the conspiracy does not need to be present at the time of the act" (Section 417, *Judicial Council of California Criminal Jury Instructions*, 2006).

In this session, we'll consider the most reasonable inference from our innate understanding of personal responsibility as we try to account for our appropriate inclination to blame or praise the actions of others.

At the criminal trial, Paul's upbringing and his drug addiction were cited by his attorney as potential explanations (or excuses) for his behavior. None of these factors were considered excusatory by the jury, however, and Paul was ultimately convicted and sentenced to state prison. The jury considered Paul's motivations (his desire to acquire money he hadn't earned in order to satisfy his free choice to continue abusing drugs) and came to the conclusion Paul made several free, uncoerced choices.

Are prosecutions of this kind fair, given the nature of our materialistic cosmos? If we live in a purely physical universe governed by the laws of physics and chemistry, do any of us truly have the freedom to make choices like the ones Paul and Sandy made? In this session, we'll examine the existence of "free agency" to see if the freedom we seem to experience can be explained by staying *inside* the "room" of the universe.

OPEN THE CASE FILE

(5 MINUTES – CONSIDER AND ANSWER AS MANY QUESTIONS AS POSSIBLE)

Think about some of the bad choices you've made in the past. List a couple in the spaces below, along with the driving forces and contributing factors that led you to make those choices:

Bad Decision: Factors That Contributed to the Bad Decision:

_____   _____

_____   _____

                               _____

_____   _____

_____   _____

                               _____

 Review some of the factors you listed above that contributed to your bad decisions. How many of these factors were dictated by or predicated on your ability (or the ability of *others*) to choose *freely*, either during the decision-making process or prior to the point of decision?

_____

_____

_____

Read Matthew 3:2, Matthew 4:17, and Acts 3:19. Why does repentance require the ability for each of us to act *freely*?

_____

_____

_____

VIEW THE VIDEO TESTIMONY
(10 MINUTES - TAKE NOTES)

Examining a criminal case involving free agency

_____

_____

_____

Understanding the limitations that a purely physical universe would place on free agency

_____

_____

_____

Listing four things we could not experience without free agency

_____

_____

_____

Investigating efforts to deny free agency altogether

_____

_____

_____

Examining the efforts to stay *inside* the "room" of the universe to explain free agency

"Quantum" theories:

_____

_____

"Emergence" theories:

_____

_____

Investigating the reasonable explanation of a creative Mind *outside* the "room" of the universe:

_____

_____

_____

CONDUCT A GROUP INVESTIGATION
(25 MINUTES – INVESTIGATE THE ISSUES AND ANSWER THE QUESTIONS)

Read the following paragraph aloud:

Nonmaterial minds don't exist in a purely material universe. All events (including Paul's decision to commit the burglary) are simply physical events governed by the laws of physics; these events have prior material causes that made their occurrence *inevitable*. Paul's decisions, if we live in a purely material universe, were determined by prior causal events beyond his control. His apparent "choices" were nothing more than dominoes falling in a long line of dominoes—single events in a series of prior physical events, brain synapses firing in response to prior brain events. In the video, J. Warner described two efforts to stay *inside* the "room" of the universe to account for our experience of free agency. Read two more "naturalistic" explanations and answer the following questions as a group:

Is Our *Definition* of Free Will Incorrect?

As we've seen in other efforts to change important definitions to stay *inside* the "room" for an explanation, some philosophers simply *redefine the concept* of free will. Philosopher Harry Frankfurt, for example, accepts that our basic ("first-order") desires (such as the desire to eat a hamburger or read this book) may be dictated by physical, material processes in our brains. But he believes that if we *agree* with these desires (our approval is described as a "second-order" desire), this agreement could be described as "free will."

A Tool for the Call-Out Bag:

HOW MUCH EVIDENCE DOES IT TAKE TO REFUTE EYEWITNESS TESTIMONY?

When an eyewitness makes an observation and reports it to an investigator, evidence is typically required if we hope to refute his or her testimony. When several witnesses report the same observation, the level of needed evidence rises dramatically.

All of us, as humans, witness our own free wills as we make decisions and freely choose actions. If our collective eyewitness observations are to be refuted, the evidence to the contrary will have to be overwhelming. If it isn't, we can reasonably trust our observations.

1. Does Frankfurt's "hierarchal" description of decision making seem to accurately describe your real free-will experiences? Why, or why not?

_____

_____

_____

2. Even if physical processes determine our "first-order" desires, what would be required for us to *agree* with those impulses? Given this requirement, why does this explanation of free agency *fail*?

_____

_____

_____

Is Free Will Simply an *Illusion*?

Many atheists, such as philosopher and neuroscientist Sam Harris, reject free will altogether and describe it as an *illusion*. While this approach is certainly logically consistent with an atheistic worldview, it doesn't adequately account for the evidence of *our own experience*. If atheists hope to convince us that free will is an *illusion*, they are going to need some evidence to do so rather than simply relying on their philosophically natural presuppositions.

3. Denying the existence of free will has consequences. Name some of these consequences:

_____

_____

_____

4. Even if free agency is an illusion, is it possible to live as though none of us is free to make choices? Why, or why not?

_____

_____

_____

5. Examine the tool offered in this section for your "Call-Out Bag." Why should our *experience* of free will overrule any effort to deny it exists?

_____

_____

_____

Examine the following diagram that illustrates the four ways atheists try to explain free agency from *inside* the "room" of the natural universe. Work together to provide reasons for why these explanations fail:

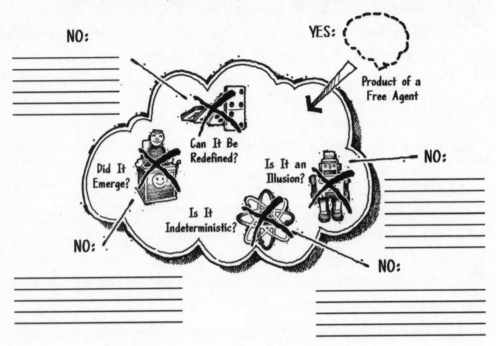

"Inside the Room" or "Outside the Room"
The Weakness of Internal Explanations Compared to the Strength of External Explanations

TAKE A PERSONAL ASSESSMENT
(4 MINUTES – EXAMINE YOUR OWN SITUATION AND ANSWER THE QUESTIONS)

As humans, each one of us has a *dual* nature. We have brains, but we also have *minds*. Criminal courts in America recognize our dual nature. Courts consider a defendant's ability as a "practical reasoner"—his or her ability, given a normal functioning brain, to make decisions and cause actions. Courts, therefore, recognize the role of the physical, material brain in this decision-making process. If the defendant's brain has been damaged by a lesion, injury, stroke, or neurotransmitter disorder, he or she may be considered less culpable based on diminished capacity. Consider your own life or the lives of people you know:

Describe a time in your life (or a time in the life of someone you know) when your (or someone else's) physical limitations may have impacted the choices you (or that person) made:

_____

_____

_____

 How might you (or the person you know) have overcome these physical limitations to better achieve the desired goal?

_____

_____

_____

Think of a friend or family member who is suffering from a brain injury or disease (like Alzheimer's or dementia). Given what you now know about the legal considerations related to *physical* brain limitations and *mental* free choices, how will this information help you understand, empathize, and interact with people who are suffering from brain damage or disease?

_____

_____

_____

 **FORM A STRATEGIC PLAN**
(5 MINUTES – EXAMINE YOUR CALENDAR AND CREATE AN ACTION PLAN)

The case for free agency is strong and can be easily articulated to your friends or family members who are skeptical of God's existence. Take the following steps to prepare yourself to share this important evidence with someone you know:

Someone I know who would benefit from this evidence: _____

Set a date to talk with that person: _____

Prepare for the conversation by reviewing the diagram in this session, then do your best to fill in the "suspect" profile, given all the evidence we've collected so far.

 Following the conversation, list the objections this person gave if he or she resisted the notion that free agency is impossible under a material, atheistic view of the universe:

_____

_____

_____

 How might you establish a plan to better prepare yourself to answer these objections?

_____

_____

_____

Our Emerging "Suspect" Profile:

WHAT IS THE NATURE OF OUR "SUSPECT"?

Given what we know so far, the cause of the universe is:

1. external to the _____

2. non_____, a_____, and non_____

3. un_____

4. powerful enough to _____ everything we see in the universe

5. specifically purposeful enough to produce a universe _____ for life

6. intelligent and _____

7. _____ and resourceful

8. a conscious Mind

9. free to choose (and create) personally

 ## MAKE A CLOSING STATEMENT
(1 MINUTE – CONTEMPLATE AND PRAY)

Free will is difficult to deny (unless, of course, we have the freedom to deny it). Attempts to account for free will from "inside the room" require us to redefine what we mean by "free will," embrace it as the mysterious product of emergence, or attribute it to quantum physics. None of these explanations are adequate. If, however, free will can be attributed to an external source capable of creating humans with consciousness and the freedom to make personal decisions, we could adequately explain our collective experience of free agency.

Dear Lord, free agency is a gift from You. It allows us to love You and love others. We make decisions and we know there is a connection between our actions and the resulting consequences. As we consider our options, we have the ability to think and deliberate. Our thoughts aren't constrained by physical events, causes, or processes. Our ability to choose means that we can make the choice to accept Christ, to choose good instead of evil, and to freely trust Your promises for the future. Thank You for Your grace and patience with us, amen.

CONDUCT A SECONDARY INVESTIGATION
(READ ON YOUR OWN FOR BETTER UNDERSTANDING)

This session was developed from *God's Crime Scene* chapter 6, "Free Will or Full Wiring: Are Real Choices Even Possible?" For a deeper understanding of the evidence for free agency and the inference of a divine, immaterial "Free Agent" *outside* the "room" of the natural universe, read and take notes on the Secondary Investigation section of *God's Crime Scene* (pages 250–59).

_____

_____

_____

_____

_____

_____

_____

_____

_____

_____

_____

LAW AND ORDER

Is Morality More Than an Opinion?

Jesse was known as "Smiley" to his fellow gang members, but he wasn't smiling now. As a member of one of the largest street gangs in Los Angeles County—with membership exceeding ten thousand—he was used to being contacted by the police. Today, however, would likely be the last time he would have a conversation with a police officer. I arrested Jesse for the murder of a rival gang member who'd made a sexually suggestive remark to Jesse's sister a week earlier.

I'd been working the gang detail for over a year, and I'd spent two days searching for Jesse in this neighborhood. While Jesse was not a resident of our community, his victim was. Jesse drove into our town, found the rival gangster who made the suggestive remark to his sister, and gleefully tortured his victim until he died from his injuries.

I was a committed atheist at the time of Jesse's arrest, but the episode caused me to consider the moral status of Jesse's crime. Was Jesse morally justified in torturing the man who offended his sister? Jesse's fellow gang members certainly thought so, and Jesse later confessed he enjoyed committing the assault. This form of "street justice" was common between these two sets of rivals. They obeyed a moral code all their own.

Are all moral truths (even those we accept as law-abiding citizens) simply the product of cultural perspective or personal preference? If so, which segment of the culture—and which set of individuals—gets to decide what's morally acceptable?

For many of us, the existence of transcendent, objective moral truth seems rather self-evident. To "supersize" the point, all of us would agree it's never morally acceptable to torture babies *for the fun of it*. For that matter, it's never morally acceptable to torture *anyone* for the *fun of it* (including the man who offended Jesse's sister). This is a transcendent, objective moral truth claim; it applies to all of us, regardless of *who we are, where we are* on the planet, and *when we've lived* in history.

There are a number of similar transcendent, objective moral virtues accepted by humans throughout history, even though these are sometimes nuanced by circumstances. As Oxford scholar C. S. Lewis said, "Men have differed as regards what people you ought to be unselfish to—whether it was only your own family, or your fellow countrymen, or every one. But they have always agreed that you ought not to put yourself first. Selfishness has never been admired."[1]

Moral truths of this nature are more than simple claims; they are *obligations* between *persons*. As a police officer, I am not morally obligated to my police car, but I am morally obligated to the officer sitting *next* to me in the car. Similarly, I'm not morally obligated to space, time, matter, or the laws of physics and chemistry.

Is it possible to account for transcendent, objective, and *obligatory* moral truths from inside the "room" of the physical universe? In this session, we'll examine this question to see if the best explanation for such truths is a transcendent, personal, moral authority *outside* the "room" of the universe.

Cold-Case Approach:

HOW DO LEGAL HIERARCHIES HELP US DETERMINE THE SOURCE OF ULTIMATE AUTHORITY?

Police officers and detectives must learn the hierarchy of laws in a variety of jurisdictions based on the region in which they work:

Local, Municipal Codes: laws and codes created by city governments. They typically govern local concerns and interests.

Regional, State Penal Codes: laws created and enforced within the borders of a state. They typically address more serious crimes common to local jurisdictions.

National, Federal Laws: statutes created by the federal government. They typically address issues of interstate commerce or the protection of civil rights or issues related to the fair collection of taxes.

In this session, we'll examine a similar hierarchy of moral authority to determine if moral laws are simply "local," "regional," or "national." If moral truths transcend all these levels of authority, from where might they come?

OPEN THE CASE FILE
(5 MINUTES – CONSIDER AND ANSWER AS MANY QUESTIONS AS POSSIBLE)

Think about the last time someone harmed you in some way. Who committed the moral violation, and what was the nature of the offense?

_____

_____

_____

1 Why was it morally wrong for this person to do what he or she did?

_____

_____

_____

2 Imagine confronting the person who offended you. What would you say if that person told you that, in his or her opinion, he or she did nothing wrong?

_____

_____

_____

3 What would you say if that same person told you that he or she had been raised by a family (or community) who also believed there was no harm in doing what he or she did?

_____

_____

_____

VIEW THE VIDEO TESTIMONY
(11 MINUTES – TAKE NOTES)

Reviewing the moral "hierarchy" and the story of Jesse

_____

_____

_____

_____

_____

? How-High Does the Moral Hierarchy Extend?

United Nations Declarations

United States Federal Laws

California State Laws

Los Angeles Municipal Codes

Jesse's Gang's Decrees

Jesse's Personal Beliefs

Examining the existence of objective, transcendent moral laws (by adding "for the fun of it")

_____

_____

_____

Searching for the "foundation" of objective moral laws

_____

Individuals?

_____

_____

_____

Groups of individuals?

_____

_____

_____

Investigating the nature of moral *obligations*

_____

_____

_____

Examining the goal of "human flourishing" as the source of objective moral truth

_____

_____

_____

_____

CONDUCT A GROUP INVESTIGATION
(24 MINUTES – INVESTIGATE THE ISSUES AND ANSWER THE QUESTIONS)

Can we explain and account for obligatory moral truths from *inside* the "room" of the physical universe? Read the following alternative explanations aloud, and work together as a group to answer the associated questions:

Are Moral Truths an Illusion?

Some atheists believe moral statements don't describe what the universe is *like* but instead describe how humans *feel about things* in the universe. According to "logical positivists," if a statement can't be verified or falsified by observation or perception, it can't be claimed true or false. This approach eliminates the need to account for moral truth by simply eliminating our ability to talk about it. But this redefinition of truth presumes the only kinds of facts we can examine are facts related to physical objects or events.

 1 Why does this explanation fail to account for objective moral truths? What would you say to someone who claims a moral concept or truth isn't as real as a physical object or material event?

_____

_____

_____

 Are Moral Truths Simply Brute Facts about the Universe?

Some philosophers recognize the existence of objective, transcendent moral truths but simply account for them by describing them as "fixed features" of the universe (like math facts or the laws of logic).

2 While this explanation might explain the existence of a moral *law*, why doesn't it explain the existence of moral *obligations*? What did J. Warner say was required for a moral *obligation*?

_____

_____

_____

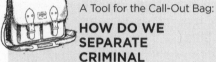

A Tool for the Call-Out Bag:

HOW DO WE SEPARATE CRIMINAL EVIDENCE FROM NONCRIMINAL PROPERTY?

In every crime scene there exist pieces of evidence left by the suspect and property belonging to the victim. Detectives have to learn how to distinguish between the two so they won't mistake as evidence something belonging to the victim.

If a woman is killed while living alone, for example, and detectives find a man's shoe print at the scene of the murder, they would have good reason to suspect the print is evidence rather than an artifact from the victim. The very nature of an item may distinguish it from the environment in which it is found and require us to explain how it got there.

In a similar way, the nature of moral truth distinguishes it from the material, causal nature of the universe. Why would a material universe contain objective moral truths and obligations? Moral truth is distinct from the environment in which it exists. It requires us to explain how it got there.

Are Moral Truths a Product of Individual Belief?

Some philosophers believe all moral truths are *subjective* rather than *objective*. According to this view (termed "moral subjectivism"), morality varies from person to person. Moral truths are simply personal *opinions* or *feelings*, and if there are no transcendent moral truths, there is no need for a transcendent moral truth *source*.

Read Isaiah 5:20:

Woe to those who call evil good, and good evil; who substitute darkness for light and light for darkness; who substitute bitter for sweet and sweet for bitter!

What is the danger in trusting one's personal opinions or feelings?

_____

_____

_____

Why does moral subjectivism make it impossible to distinguish what one person considers morally virtuous from what another considers morally vile?

_____

_____

_____

Are Moral Truths a Product of Culture?

Some philosophers attribute moral truths to societies and cultures. Philosophers who accept this view are called "moral relativists." They believe people groups create their own moral codes rather than discover them.

Why does this approach make it impossible for any one group to logically argue for the "rightness" of a moral position over another group?

_____

_____

_____

Are Moral Truths Human-Specific Biological Facts?

According to Sam Harris, *well-being* (also described as "human flourishing") is the purpose of our existence as human beings. Since human biology transcends human culture, moral truths (if they are rooted in human *biology*) would also transcend culture.

But Harris believes that a certain *kind* of existence represents "human flourishing," involving certain virtues and values on the part of humans. Why do these moral *requirements* related to "human flourishing" disqualify his explanation for the existence of moral truths?

_____

_____

_____

Our Emerging "Suspect" Profile:

WHAT IS THE NATURE OF OUR "SUSPECT"?

Given what we know so far, the cause of the universe is:

1. external to the universe

2. nonspatial, atemporal, and nonmaterial

3. uncaused

4. powerful enough to create everything we see in the universe

5. specifically purposeful enough to produce a universe fine-tuned for life

6. intelligent and communicative

7. creative and resourceful

8. a conscious Mind

9. free to choose (and create) personally

10. the personal source of moral truth and obligation

TAKE A PERSONAL ASSESSMENT
(4 MINUTES – EXAMINE YOUR OWN SITUATION AND ANSWER THE QUESTIONS)

Some of the explanations for objective moral truth from *inside* the "room" of the universe can be complex and even a bit confusing. Which of the five explanations we've examined in this session is most difficult to understand?

_____

How can you increase your understanding of this explanation so you can better respond to someone who might offer it as an objection to the necessity of God as a transcendent, objective moral truth giver?

_____

_____

_____

 Briefly fill in the diagram below, testing your own ability to explain why efforts to account for objective moral truth from *inside* the "room" of the universe are weaker than those from *outside* the "room":

"Inside the Room" or "Outside the Room"
The Weakness of Internal Explanations Compared to the Strength of External Explanations

NO:

_____

YES: Grounded in a Personal, Transcendent, Moral Being

NO:

_____

_____

_____

Illusions?

Brute Facts?

Purely Subjective?

Relative to Groups?

Biological Facts?

NO:

_____

_____

NO:

_____

_____

FORM A STRATEGIC PLAN
(5 MINUTES – EXAMINE YOUR CALENDAR AND CREATE AN ACTION PLAN)

The best training often requires a training partner. As we get ready to complete this eight-session study, pick someone with whom you can partner as we prepare to use what we've learned to communicate the truth to others.

1. Identify someone as a training partner: _____

   Set a date to meet *following* the last session of the study: _____

2. Identify three areas of study you can further examine as partners:

   _____

   _____

   _____

Read the following verses *prior* to the first meeting with your training partner:

Proverbs 27:17

Ecclesiastes 4:9

John 15:4–5

Ephesians 2:10

What do these verses tell you about the value of a training partner?

_____

_____

MAKE A CLOSING STATEMENT
(1 MINUTE – CONTEMPLATE AND PRAY)

As philosophers David Baggett and Jerry Walls observed, "Persons with intrinsic value and dignity seem much less likely to emerge from valueless impersonal stuff than from the intentional hand of a personal Creator."[2] If humans were created in the image of this Creator, our position *inside* the "room" would indeed be worthy of moral obligation, and a Creator such as this could also provide a proper explanation for moral truth. Moral obligations exist between *persons*; if moral laws are transcendent, it seems reasonable for us to look for the transcendent *person* to whom we are ultimately obligated. Transcendent moral laws require a transcendent moral law source, and an all-powerful, nonmaterial, nonspatial, atemporal, purposeful, personal Creator would certainly qualify.

Dear Lord, transcendent, objective moral laws have been accepted by humans throughout history, and these moral truths, guidelines, and obligations assume the inherent dignity of all human beings. They also require a source. You, oh Lord, are that source. You are THE lawgiver. You love us enough to guide us and protect us with a standard of righteousness, even though You know we will never be able to obey Your laws perfectly. Thank You for forgiving our failures as we allow Your moral law to guide us and reveal our need for a Savior. Thank You, Lord, for Your loving-kindness and infinite wisdom. In Your love we pray, amen.

CONDUCT A SECONDARY INVESTIGATION
(READ ON YOUR OWN FOR BETTER UNDERSTANDING)

This session examines the evidence described in *God's Crime Scene* chapter 7, "Law and Order: Is Morality More Than an Opinion?" For an in-depth discussion of why moral laws are best grounded in the existence of a transcendent, personal moral lawgiver *outside* the "room" of the natural universe, read the Secondary Investigation section of *God's Crime Scene* (pages 260–71).

_____

_____

_____

_____

_____

_____

_____

_____

_____

_____

_____

_____

_____

Session Eight / Closing Argument
THE EVIDENCE OF EVIL
Can God and Evil Coexist?

Jackie Corbin was eight years old in 1980 when she was kidnapped on the street in front of her home. Her parents were cooking Christmas dinner. They didn't see what happened to her, and she couldn't hear their calls as they desperately searched for her into the evening hours. Two days later, officers discovered her body lying in a field north of Los Angeles County. The murder mobilized everyone in our police department. Over four hundred leads were developed in the first two weeks. A suspect, Francis Denny, was ultimately arrested.

Denny was twenty-two years old at the time—a seemingly distant (and often quiet) loner, but acquainted with Jackie's family. Denny was disconnected and dispassionate in his interviews, and this led detectives to believe he was hiding something. When they told him the gruesome details of Jackie's death, Denny seemed unconcerned.

It's difficult to understand how anyone could respond so calmly to the descriptions offered by detectives, and I can understand why investigators suspected Denny, given his apparently uncaring responses. But as it turned out, Francis Denny didn't commit the crime for which he was accused. Detectives eventually discovered that Denny was attending a movie on the day of the murder and was unavailable to commit the crime. The murder of Jackie Corbin is still an open, unsolved case.

When I first started investigating the existence of God, I suspected the stubborn presence of evil and injustice would ultimately eliminate the reasonable existence of such a Being, in the same way Denny's alibi eliminated him from suspicion. Perhaps the most obvious and pervasive reality of the universe is the existence of evil and injustice. Most of us, even as casual investigators, have had personal contact with this form of evidence. If we are prepared to look *outside* the "room" of the universe for a "suspect" to explain the seven pieces of evidence we've examined so far, we must also account for the presence of evil and injustice with this same "suspect."

If the Creator of the universe is powerful enough to create everything from nothing, this Creator is most certainly powerful enough to eliminate all imperfection, including *moral* imperfection. Such a perfectly "good" Creator would, therefore, be a reasonable source for the moral virtues we recognize in our universe. But does the degree of evil we see *inside* the "room" contradict the nature of a Divine Creator?

If the morally benevolent, all-powerful Divine Creator of the universe we've described from the evidence in prior chapters does indeed exist, how are we to explain the existence of evil *inside* the "room" of the universe? In this session, we'll investigate this last piece of evidence to see if it eliminates the reasonable existence of God, or simply adds to the case for His existence. We'll also develop a final "suspect profile" to assemble what we've learned and reveal the nature of the "suspect" responsible for God's "crime scene."

Cold-Case Approach:

WHAT IS EXCULPATORY EVIDENCE?

When assessing the involvement of a particular suspect in a crime, there are three possible forms of evidence related to the suspect's guilt:

Inculpatory Evidence: evidence that tends to confirm the suspect's involvement in the crime.

Exculpatory Evidence: evidence that indicates the defendant did not commit the crime.

Irrelevant Evidence: evidence that is neither exculpatory nor inculpatory (and is likely to be excluded from a trial).

There are many forms of exculpatory evidence, including testimony from someone supporting the suspect's alibi and forensic evidence (such as fingerprints or DNA) eliminating the suspect. Exculpatory evidence may be direct or circumstantial, in the form of testimony or in the form of physical exhibits presented in court.

In this session, we'll examine a potential piece of exculpatory evidence to see if it eliminates the "suspect" we've developed so far.

OPEN THE CASE FILE
*(5 MINUTES – CONSIDER AND ANSWER AS MANY
QUESTIONS AS POSSIBLE)*

Most of us have experienced evil personally or have at least *observed* it in the world around us. In the following spaces, list evils you have experienced or observed, and the *causes* for these evils.

Evil that occurred: Cause behind the evil event (the reason why it happened):

_____   _____

_____   _____

                                     _____

_____   _____

_____   _____

                                     _____

_____   _____

                                     _____

                                     _____

Now examine your list. Which of these evil occurrences is hardest to understand, given the existence of an all-powerful, all-loving God?

_____

Why would God allow such a thing to occur? What would you tell a nonbeliever?

_____

_____

VIEW THE VIDEO TESTIMONY
(13 MINUTES – TAKE NOTES)

Answering the question: "Why did this happen to my loved one?"

_____

_____

_____

Assembling the causes for Jackie's murder

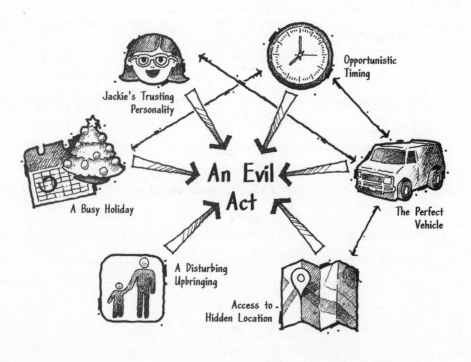

_____

_____

_____

_____

Reviewing the evidence we've examined so far

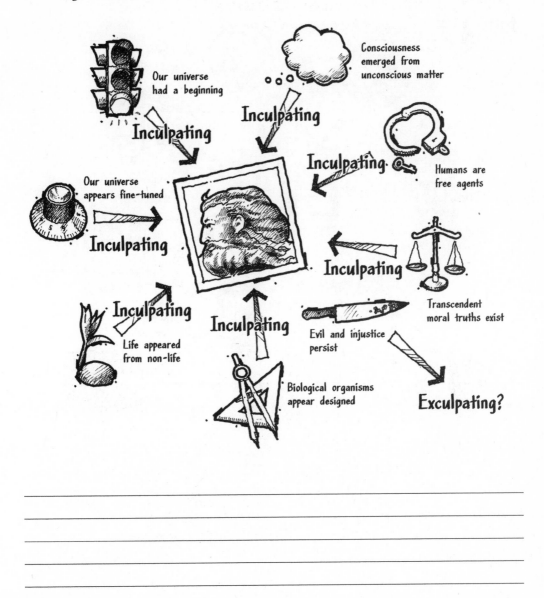

Assembling the cumulative explanations for why God might allow any act of evil

_____

_____

_____

_____

_____

Establishing an accurate view of eternity

_____

_____

_____

_____

_____

Asking why we call it "evil" in the first place

_____

_____

_____

Examining our final "suspect" profile

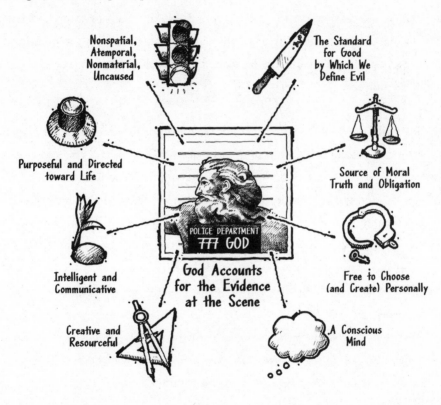

_____

_____

_____

_____

CONDUCT A GROUP INVESTIGATION
(22 MINUTES – INVESTIGATE THE ISSUES AND ANSWER THE QUESTIONS)

In the video, J. Warner examined one reason why an all-powerful, all-loving God would allow evil: *an accurate view of eternity.* Divide your group into pairs or teams and assign the following six descriptive paragraphs to these teams. Work to answer the questions, then return to the group and share your answers related to these six reasons why God would allow suffering in the universe:

1. Evil Can Be Reconciled If We Have a Proper Reverence for Free Agency

Love requires freedom; no true expression of love has ever been coerced. As we discussed in session 6, rationality *also* requires freedom. If the Divine Creator of the universe respects freedom as much as we do, we should expect a beautiful universe in which love and reason are possible, even though hate and irrationality must also be tolerated and allowed (at least in this mortal portion of our existence).

Read Mark 7:21–22:

For from within, out of the heart of men, proceed the evil thoughts, fornications, thefts, murders, adulteries, deeds of coveting and wickedness, as well as deceit, sensuality, envy, slander, pride and foolishness.

Why do you think we often choose to commit evil, and why is this freedom a necessary (although dangerous) requirement for love to be possible? How does the requirement of *free agency* help explain why we see evil in the world?

_____

_____

_____

2. Evil Can Be Reconciled If We Hold an Appropriate Definition of Love

Our definition of love has been deeply compromised by the way it is portrayed in contemporary novels and movies. Love is far more than sentimentality, romance, or affection. Parents know this better than anyone else. There are times when the deepest, truest expression of love is some form of discipline or correction.

Read Hebrews 12:9–11:

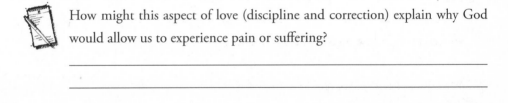

Furthermore, we had earthly fathers to discipline us, and we respected them; shall we not much rather be subject to the Father of spirits, and live? For they disciplined us for a short time as seemed best to them, but He disciplines us for our good, so that we may share His holiness. All discipline for the moment seems not to be joyful, but sorrowful; yet to those who have been trained by it, afterwards it yields the peaceful fruit of righteousness.

How might this aspect of love (discipline and correction) explain why God would allow us to experience pain or suffering?

_____

_____

_____

3. Evil Can Be Reconciled If We Understand Its Role in Character Development

Loving parents are usually more concerned with their children's character than their comfort, and character is developed more through adversity than advantage. Good character emerges in response to suffering.

Read Romans 5:3–5:

And not only this, but we also exult in our tribulations, knowing that tribulation brings about perseverance; and perseverance, proven character; and proven

character, hope; and hope does not disappoint, because the love of God has been
poured out within our hearts through the Holy Spirit who was given to us.

Why do tribulations develop character and demonstrate the love of God?

_____

_____

_____

4. Evil Can Be Reconciled If We Recognize Its Power to Draw Us

Tragedy has a way of redirecting our thoughts and pointing us to a life beyond the limits of our present experience "inside the room." If there is a loving Divine Creator who has designed us for an existence beyond the grave, it might not be unreasonable for this Creator to use hardship to refocus those of us who haven't been paying attention.

Read Romans 8:28:

And we know that God causes all things to work together for good to those
who love God, to those who are called according to His purpose.

Based on this verse, what kinds of hardships might God allow us to endure in order to accomplish His purpose?

_____

_____

_____

5. Evil Can Be Reconciled If We Accept Its Existence as a Consequence

Sometimes our suffering is simply the result of bad choices on our part, and it's not always easy to see how our prior choices eventually cause such suffering. There are times when choices we made years earlier eventually catch up with us.

Read Galatians 6:7–9:

Do not be deceived, God is not mocked; for whatever a man sows, this he will also reap. For the one who sows to his own flesh will from the flesh reap corruption, but the one who sows to the Spirit will from the Spirit reap eternal life. Let us not lose heart in doing good, for in due time we will reap if we do not grow weary.

Why might God allow us to suffer the consequences of our own bad choices and actions?

_____

_____

_____

6. Evil Can Be Reconciled If We Acknowledge Our Limited Understanding

But even with these prior explanations in mind, there are times when suffering seems entirely inexplicable. Why do bad things happen to "good" people? Why do people sometimes get away with murder? I've never investigated a case in which I was able to answer every possible question a juror might ask. In fact, the majority of my cases have been successfully prosecuted in *spite* of a number of unanswered questions. If there is a vastly superior Divine Creator, we shouldn't expect to understand every motive, every thought, or every set of concerns in the Creator's mind.

A Tool for the Call-Out Bag:

WHAT ARE WE TO DO WITH UNANSWERED QUESTIONS?

Every criminal investigation results in unanswered questions. In fact, prosecutors typically ask potential jurors if they will be able to render a decision even if they still have a few such questions. If you're the kind of person who has to know *every* detail before you can make a decision, you'll never be placed on a jury. There are no perfect cases; every case presents a quandary of one nature or another. The important issue is: Do we have enough evidence to come to a verdict *in spite of* a few unanswered questions? Unanswered questions need not prevent us from determining truth.

Read Psalm 33:13–15:

The LORD looks from heaven; He sees all the sons of men; from His dwelling place He looks out on all the inhabitants of the earth, He who fashions the hearts of them all, He who understands all their works.

If God understands how the events of *today* impact the *future*, how might this explain why He might allow evil in our lives?

_____

_____

_____

Our Emerging "Suspect" Profile:

WHAT IS THE NATURE OF OUR "SUSPECT"?

Given what we know so far, the cause of the universe is:

1. external to the universe

2. nonspatial, atemporal, and nonmaterial

3. uncaused

4. powerful enough to create everything we see in the universe

5. specifically purposeful enough to produce a universe fine-tuned for life

6. intelligent and communicative

7. creative and resourceful

8. a conscious Mind

9. free to choose (and create) personally

10. the personal source of moral truth and obligation

11. the standard for good by which we define evil

God may *allow* evil, but He is not the *cause* of evil. Instead, He is the standard of righteousness by which we *identify* evil in the first place. Just as shadows cannot exist without sunlight, true evil cannot exist unless there is a true, objective standard of "good." There are many reasons why God may allow us to suffer, but these reasons don't eliminate God as the best inference for all the other evidence we've investigated in this study.

TAKE A PERSONAL ASSESSMENT
(4 MINUTES – EXAMINE YOUR OWN SITUATION AND ANSWER THE QUESTIONS)

Contemplate the most difficult episode of suffering or pain you've experienced in your life. Briefly describe it here:

_____

Now, given what you've learned in this session, pick one (or more) of the reasons (discussed above) why God might allow evil, and describe how God may have allowed you to experience this season of life:

One of the reasons: Why God might have allowed or used the evil:

_____   _____

_____   _____

_____   _____

_____   _____

_____   _____

_____   _____

FORM A STRATEGIC PLAN
(5 MINUTES – EXAMINE YOUR CALENDAR AND CREATE AN ACTION PLAN)

The surest way to improve your skill as a defender of truth is to be *intentional*. If you're ready to become the Christian "case maker" God has designed you to be, let this study be the catalyst for your growth and development. Don't view the time you've put into these eight sessions as an *end unto themselves* but rather as the *beginning* of a new way to approach your walk as a Christian. In the last session, you were encouraged to find a partner with whom you could practice what you've learned and extend your studies beyond these eight sessions.

You've already established a date for your first meeting (refer to the last session). Now make a list of the topics you would like to master together:

_____

_____

_____

 To master the evidence more completely, take the time to read the material described in the "Conduct a Secondary Investigation" section of each session. Set a date for completing this additional reading: _____

At your first meeting with your partner, work together to fill in the attributes required for the cause of each of the eight attributes we've examined in this overall study. Use the following diagram, allowing the prompt from each piece of evidence to remind you of the "suspect" attribute necessary to account for this evidence. Do your best to respond to the prompts without referring to the "Emerging 'Suspect' Profile" call-out box in this session:

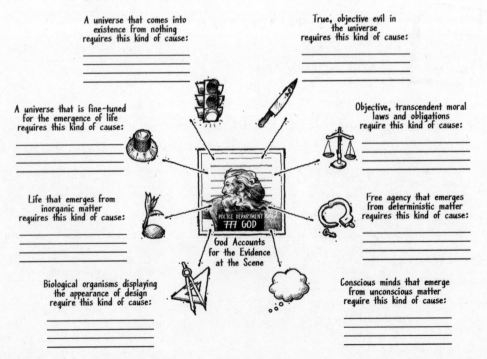

MAKE A CLOSING STATEMENT
(1 MINUTE – CONTEMPLATE AND PRAY)

Scientists and physicists have been searching for a "Theory of Everything" for decades. They'd like to unify theories of quantum mechanics (explaining physical interactions at the quantum level) and the theory of general relativity (explaining physical interactions at the macro level). They're looking for a single theory, a single explanation. It turns out there is a unified explanation for everything we see (and don't see) in our universe. It's not an impersonal set of physical properties or laws, however. It's a personal, all-powerful Divine Being.

Dear God, the love You have for us allows us the freedom to love or hate. As much as we detest the reality of evil in our lives, we know evil is actually evidence for Your existence. You, God, are the standard of all righteousness by which we measure good and evil. We pray You strengthen us against our sinful desires and use us as instruments of Your love. We know there is more than enough evidence for Your existence, and we pray for opportunities to share this evidence with others. Help us to project Your love and goodness into the world. In Jesus's name we pray, amen.

CONDUCT A SECONDARY INVESTIGATION
(READ ON YOUR OWN FOR BETTER UNDERSTANDING)

To better understand the issues raised in this final session (from *God's Crime Scene* chapter 8, "The Evidence of Evil: Can God and Evil Coexist?"), read the Secondary Investigation section of *God's Crime Scene* (pages 271–78).

_____

_____

_____

_____

_____

_____

_____

_____

_____

_____

_____

_____

_____

_____

_____

NOTES

SESSION 1: IN THE BEGINNING

1. Andrei Linde, "Cyclic Universe Runs into Criticism," *Physics World* (June 2002): 8.

2. Paul Davies, "The Birth of the Cosmos," in *God, Cosmos, Nature, and Creativity*, ed. Jill Gready (Edinburgh: Scottish Academic Press, 1995), 8–9.

SESSION 2: TAMPERING WITH THE EVIDENCE

1. Lawrence Krauss, *A Universe from Nothing: Why There Is Something Rather Than Nothing* (New York: Atria Books, 2013), Kindle ebook location 1690.

SESSION 4: SIGNS OF DESIGN

1. Richard Dawkins, *The Blind Watchmaker: Why the Evidence of Evolution Reveals a Universe without Design* (New York: W. W. Norton, 1996), 1.

2. Robert Dorit, "Biological Complexity," in *Scientists Confront Intelligent Design and Creationism*, ed. Andrew J. Petto and Laurie R. Godfrey (New York: W. W. Norton, 2007), 244.

SESSION 5: OUR EXPERIENCE OF CONSCIOUSNESS

1. David J. Chalmers, *The Conscious Mind: In Search of a Fundamental Theory* (Oxford: Oxford University Press, 1997), 3.

SESSION 7: LAW AND ORDER

1. C. S. Lewis, *Mere Christianity* (New York: HarperOne, 2001), 6.

2. David Baggett and Jerry L. Walls, *Good God: The Theistic Foundations of Morality* (Oxford: Oxford University Press, 2011), 11.

At David C Cook, we equip the local church around
the corner and around the globe to make disciples.
Come see how we are working together—go to
www.davidccook.org. Thank you!